T0068237

Something
is Eternal

Something
is Eternal

Richard Henry Orndorff

SOMETHING IS ETERNAL

iUniverse books may be ordered through booksellers or by contacting:

iUniverse
1663 Liberty Drive
Bloomington, IN 47403
www.iuniverse.com
844-349-9409

ISBN: 978-1-6632-5645-4 (sc)
ISBN: 978-1-6632-5644-7 (e)

Library of Congress Control Number: 2023917977

Print information available on the last page.

iUniverse rev. date: 11/06/2023

Contents

Dedication

To the Love of my life: Carol Jean Hammond Orndorff

and

Kim and Paul, and grandsons Owen and Brennan Paik

and

My Friends, Family, Former Students, Colleagues,

and

To the late Dr. Paul A. Payne, once my psychologist (for losing weight) at the University of Cincinnati, in the late 1980s. Dr. Payne was a graduate of Phillips University, Enid, Oklahoma, Yale Divinity School, and Ohio State University, Ph.D. He served as founding minister at Northwest Christian Church in Columbus, and then had 35-year career as a psychologist at the University of Cincinnati.

Act 3, Our Town by Thornton Wilder

"STAGE MANAGER: Now, there are some things we all know but don't take out and look at very often. We all know that something is eternal. And it ain't names, and it ain't houses, and it ain't earth, and it ain't even the stars. . .."

Foreword

Possessing the experience of observing the writings of Richard Orndorff over five decades, it is interesting to note the evolution of his writing style over time. While we all practice introspection, his expressive skill goes far beyond that base scope of awareness.

Using simulated character dialogue, he presents a realistic snapshot of the varied life choices and their many subsequent consequences that we all encounter but seldom process and externally share. His treatment of introspection enables the reader to apply personal stimuli and to process self-examination on a far deeper level.

It has been a privilege and a growth experience to have had the friendship of Richard and his wife, Carol, over these many decades.

Craig Brelsford

Preface

This is the Amorella, Richard's spiritual companion, who is, by definition, a conscious spiritual being. In his lifetime of notes, Richard once labeled me a 'Betweener' many decades ago. Richard came to think of me as Angelic and then as Archangelic in terms of ancient nomenclature for spiritual beings. Throughout this book I will be in italics when speaking.

Richard believed in Faeries, in the folklore of the British Isles, parts of Europe, and the United States. Richard loved words and took the words literarily. He was four years old. If something had a name, it was real. 'Faery' is a name, so, faeries were real.

A bit older, when at Longfellow Elementary in Westerville Schools, Richard learned about angels in Sunday School at the First Presbyterian Church at the corner of Knox and Walnut near Uptown Westerville. Still thinking literally, he adopted the angel concept because they were depicted as beautiful in artistic sketches. This is before reading mythological-like stories. Once he adapted this concept, he realized that not all names are literal.

In the upper elementary grades, Richard became interested in history because he liked the Greek and Roman mythologies. They were entertaining but also scary. At the same time, he came across one of the first historical characters of interest. Julius Caesar. He already knew about Augustus Caesar because of the stories about Jesus, who, to Richard, seemed like a decently good person who was killed for the wrong reasons. Jesus was unjustly put to death. He liked Jesus' words, "Do unto Others What You Would Do unto Yourself." The words were simple and appeared fair and just. These words were no reason to kill someone.

About this same time in upper elementary years, Richard enjoyed rummaging through the house when no one was home; he discovered several photographs hidden in a cedar chest. He had toyed with the combination lock for several weeks before happening on the combination. The photographs were of naked people. He saw a pile of something in another photograph. It took minutes before he realized this collection was scenes of nothing but naked dead people who were killed, and he could see no earthly reason for it. Richard told no one. He asked no one. The pictures sat in his mind alongside the depictions of Jesus and two other people being crucified.

Richard continued reading the histories and mythologies of Greece and Rome and hero-worshipped Julius Caesar. Caesar appeared to be a good man and a good soldier who was killed only this time by his friends, not his enemies. This seemed unjust and a callous way to be treated by friends.

When entering Emerson Junior High School, Richard had several friends, girls and boys. His oldest friend is John Douglas Goss. The two have been heart-fast friends since the fourth grade at Minerva Park Elementary School. Both boys liked science and history. Their Class of 1960 from Minerva Park was transferred to Whittier Elementary in Westerville in the fifth grade. At Whittier, Richard was back with friends from the first and second grades at Longfellow.

Once at Emerson Junior High in the seventh grade, Doug and Richard found another mutual interest: twin girls Kay and Ann Griffith. Doug liked Ann, and Richard fancied Kay. In the eighth grade, Richard found another friend for life, Fredrick James Milligan, nicknamed Fritz, who had transferred to Emerson like others in his Central College Elementary School class. Fritz liked history, as did Richard. Friends such as Doug and Fritz are sacred to his life. Oddly, Richard unconsciously associated Jesus and Julius Caesar with his friends, Doug and Fritz.

Richard was about to join the First Presbyterian Church in the eighth grade. But first, he had to learn some biblical matters. One was the Apostles' Creed. This Apostles' Creed brought about his first adult moral decision; one he has lived with ever since.

Richard discovered Jesus had gone into Hell before moving to Heaven to be with G-D and the Holy Ghost. Richard did not believe this because it could not be proved. Yet, Richard had to swear in a church, no less, that the Apostle's Creed was true. Richard could not gather the faith to believe. Under the pressure of circumstances at church that Sunday morning, he lied in front of G-D and everyone that he thought the Apostle's Creed was accurate and, therefore, valid. He did not.

"I was going to Hell, no question about it," says Richard today. "I consciously lied to G-D in front of witnesses, family, and friends. I lost my sense of faith but not truth because there was no proof Jesus had gone to Hell and risen again to Heaven. I consciously knew better. This conflict has not left my soul even today," say I, Richard Henry Orndorff, aged 81 years. This, and those terribly horrible photographs my father brought back from the army, changed my life forever.

His father, Richard Bookman Orndorff, and others of the Third Army Engineers liberated Dachau, a Hell of the worst sort. The pictures were from other camps and sent home with those who were there for the camps' liberations. Such injustice, despicable, unrighteous, and unclean moral behavior were framed in white, and those alive and now dead lived to see more of such horrors of war in photographs, films, and words, and people viewed similar scenes in the Middle East this October, 2023.

Richard: We can be a decent species, we Homo sapiens. We need to raise ourselves to show the better-like angels of our nature. We are not angelic beings. We are not built perfectly, but we are built to survive beyond our more common instincts.

Amorella: I was not expecting Richard to say anything in the Preface. Richard defies me, you see, by speaking a piece here and earlier when I suggested beforehand, that he kindly be patient and wait a bit. Like his father's father, Clell Tullar Orndorff, one of the kindest of men, might easily have said of young Richard, "The boy just doesn't give a tinker's damn." As an old man, Richard still doesn't give a damn. That's his shell, always has been. Other people in the world are like Richard, that's the reason he meets a good example of humanity. He is imperfect, and as such a perfectly good example of someone who needs to be dug up while he's still alive.

Why? Well, for one, his indifference allows me to exist within. I, the Amorella, am truly a Spirit. Richard writes for me. I have no physical properties. Even human ghosts, and they exist, have physical properties. When a human dies, she or he keeps an unselfishly spirit for other human spirits to witness. The Reader's spirit without the physics, acquires a sense of unselfishness and keeps her or his face at most any age she or he wishes to be seen by others, mostly friends and family, friends first. As T. S. Eliot once penned, 'There will be a time to prepare a face to meet those faces that you meet.'

In this book, we meet Richard at a much earlier age. One has to be born before she or he can die, and physical death comes to one and all, and I, the Amorella, don't mince words.

A bit more background to this work. I asked Richard to define muse and spirit in the Oxford-American Dictionary and we simplified the definitions to those that fit the circumstances in Something is Eternal.

1. *A* **muse** *is a personified force, a source of inspiration.*

2. *A* **spirit** *is the nonphysical part of a person, the seat of emotions, character and soul capable of surviving physical death;' and implied in Something is Eternal. The spirit, Amorella, is a "Helper Spirit" to the recently dead.*

3. *Richard stated that the* <u>key</u> *to this connection of muse and spirit is "the development and use of self-hypnosis" studied and learned by Richard under the instruction of the psychologist, Dr. Paul A. Payne, at the University of Cincinnati in the mid to late 1980s. Below is the Wikipedia definition of self-hypnosis that fits the context of the word in this book. The added brackets below are to individualize the definition in Richard's setting.*

Self-hypnosis or **auto-hypnosis** (as distinct from hetero-hypnosis) is a form, a process, or the result of a self-induced hypnotic state.

Frequently, self-hypnosis is used as a vehicle to enhance the efficacy of self-suggestion; and, in such cases, the subject, [Richard], "plays the dual role of suggester and suggestee".

The nature of the auto-suggestive practice may be, at one extreme, *"concentrative"*, wherein "all attention is so totally focused on (the words of the auto-suggestive formula, e.g. "Every day, in every way, I'm getting better and better") that everything else is kept out of awareness" and, at the other, *"inclusive"*, wherein subject

[Richard] "allows all kinds of thoughts, emotions, memories, and the like, to drift into their [his] consciousness".

Wikipedia

Amorella: Something is Eternal shows Richard's commentary while responding to self-hypnosis gathering information into his conscious mind throughout this work. Richard's few lifetime friends, the Readers, along with his sister, Cathy, have read this work and find his remarks honest. His words reflect the Richard H. Orndorff, four of the first readers have known over fifty-five years.

OPEN

Acknowledgments

This book is complete within the kindness of these immediate First Reader friends listed below.

Craig and Alta Brelsford, The Reverend Dr. John Douglas Goss, Frederick James Milligan, Kimberly and Paul Paik, James and Jeanne Shoemaker, Cathy, and Tod Stoessner, and The Amorella Spirit of the Forty Years, I thank them for kindly putting up with me. I am much more appreciative of their friendships than words can express.

Richard / Dad

And,

A THANK YOU TO MY OLD FRIEND

The Reverend Dr. John Douglas Goss, Ph.D. Nuclear Physics, Ohio State University; a friend for seventy-three years now; for being my Science Advisor on this Singular Project.

Prologue

By The Amorella

"This book details Richard's life, development, and accomplishments. He was born prematurely. He weighed a little under two pounds and needed to follow nourishment regulations from birth through Kindergarten. Richard also had balance and motor control complications, which were controlled by leg braces when learning to walk. And, though he was learning the alphabet and words in his late twos and threes. He did not speak in words and sentences until his early threes. His first vocal words were directed to his mother's mother, Mae Freeman Schick, the words were: "I want a cookie." His mother, Mary Laverna Schick Orndorff, was the witness. Richard's first outside interest had been his blue and white blanket, which he took with him everywhere, and his unique interest in the shapes of the letters of the alphabet. Later, he thought of individual letters as living beings and projected them as such in his silent imagination. The letters would quietly talk to him, and he would quietly talk back.

At eighty-one, Richard is reflecting on the essential matters of his life. I, his imaginary Muse from his forties when he taught British Literature, helped him create and write several books. He formally named me, "The Amorella". He misunderstood, another common mistake the man makes, and came to feel I was an Angel of G-D. This has since been clarified: I am not an Angel of G-D. I am a Spirit though. I am an Amorella, one of a collective group of one, called The Amorella.

Richard didn't believe me but he grew curious. Richard does not accept much of what he sees and hears. He's not alone. Richard has constantly consciously observed and studied his not sunlight. I do not recollect anyone asking before touching under the hospital lights. The staff just did as they wished, thus keeping me alive. Reflecting on that event, whether I controlled the situation as in the womb, events sometimes move differently than one wishes.

First, when barely conscious, I did favor human creatures' eyes. Quickly, nourishment became a necessity, like breathing. I quickly came to appreciate eye contact, gentle touching, and automatic sucking; connection and touching were the first aspects of living that offered pleasure. I didn't particularly enjoy being wrapped and/or unwrapped with a small nondescript blanket. I don't consciously remember anything about urination, defecation, or even a diaper during the first year. I moved my arms, legs, fingers, and toes, and I slept, apparently in a conscious state. Consciousness involves touch, sight, sound, smell, and taste for stimuli. That's what I learned later.

I accepted water and milk from whatever sources and first foods, whatever they were. Eating, like drinking, was necessary, but it quickly became a pleasure of warm or cool liquid and a mush of semi-solids. Somewhere between the first and second year, I became conscious of warm urination and feces discharge of mostly semi-solids into a coarse cloth wrapped and pinned above my belly button and upper leg appendages and the consciousness of both at once. Life became an irritation. I wanted to be left alone, but my body, which felt separate from me, did not.

I was never a personal pronoun. I was who I am today, now in my eighth decade. I is a noun. My other three nouns are Richard Henry Orndorff. If I pronounce "I is a pronoun," I accept this as a grammatical statement of fact, but when I say "I," meaning myself, I is a noun, not a pronoun. My full natural proper name is "I, Richard Henry Orndorff." This way of thinking became the beginning of my existence as two consciousnesses. This conditional, with maturity, has become my inner separation of a spiritual being and a physical being, each in the form of a most private separate set of consciousnesses. With the world being what it is, this meant I had to keep this self-concept an utmost secret, which I did, until the present, because this sense of honesty should be explained while I am living.

I preferred the diapers and blankets to be spotless in those early days. As I became more conscious about what life was all about, I liked my white and yellow plastic duck, which was slightly larger than my fist, and my proportionally sized blue blanket. Over the next few years, I grew attached to that blue blanket. In my twos, Mother's touch grew more critical because I was attempting to take a hand in my upbringing. I began enjoying my space, a few unmemorable toys, and wonderfully allotted quiet time for observation, contemplation, and consideration. At three, I was learning numbers and letters sometimes while Mother and I listened to her several records of show tunes and classical music. Mother took as much pleasure in reading her books as she did for me. This was not a bother. Sometimes, I listened to the novelty in the music while Mother read; I was okay with whatever she decided to do. I liked the shared space between us. The distance was tangible and visible. A playground of thought and consideration rested between my mother and me. Later, I realized the act of contemplation is spiritual because it was not easily sensed until the idea could be condensed into either sound and/or words. A bit later, I considered the brain genuine and the mind spiritual. That's how I divided the world. Imagination came first because I didn't know any better. I assumed it was spiritual because it was invisible until I did something about it. Today, I consider imagination a weak form of both spiritual and physical. When I look at conditions in the physical world, they can be both imaginative and spiritual.

By three years of age, several matters entered my consciousness. First, looking at pictures and letters is fun and exciting because of the shapes and, strangely, the empty spaces between their individual forms. Mother introduced the alphabet to me in my twos, and after learning the letters in my threes, she slowly revealed how the alphabet letters linked into words. Letters morphing into words gave me a challenging interest. In my late twos, I imagined individual letters as living and conscious form-beings like people. This I kept secret. Letters, words, and the spaces in between became special friends with which my imagination could communicate. Each letter was like a doll. A group of alphabet letters with meaning became a clothed doll in my third year. Letters and words were as good as, if not better, than children's toys.

The standard letter, 'i,' still today shows me a picture of both a spiritual and a physical reality. The dot is spiritual because it is where my head and the mind are. The stick below represents my body. I was pretty skinny and small in those days, "a skinned rabbit" in my father's eyes, at least that's what he told people at the time. Later, in my late threes, I learned this fact from Grandmother Schick, who thought it was terrible he would say such a thing. I thought the comment was honest but funny because I didn't have rabbit ears, which meant Father was making up a story. In those early years, spirituality meant almost anything invisible was also a reality.

Later, I realized my spiritual self is where my sense of consciousness exists. When Mother said, "invisible," I thought ghost-like and spiritual. Today, I feel imagination is the crossroads between spiritual and physical realities. I heard the word "crossroads" in Sunday school. That was an easy concept because our Presbyterian Church is at the corner of Knox Street and West College, a physical crossroad. An example of a spiritual hub in those days was the cross Jesus was nailed or tied to. The road led to his death or resurrection. I was told Jesus came down from the cross, but if he was tied or nailed, I didn't understand how that could be. As usual, I kept my mouth shut because I was taught it was not polite to ask foolish questions.

A spiritual crossroad is not a road but a cross that can appear as a physical crossroad. The cross has four inner corners but no outer ones. The outer corners are invisible and can be filled in by imagination. That was my thinking approach, my operandi. I did not know the word operandi in those days; we had not been formally introduced, but I did understand my method of thinking was somewhat unorthodox, so I kept it to myself as long as I saw validity in doing so. Whatever I was searching for as a child and an adult must be accurate enough to realize. Through observation and intuition, I discovered that borders on the invisible, like the outer corners of the cross, are the spiritual parts. This, of course, is looking at that inexperienced word through an eighty-year-old. A child's reality is the birthplace of the adult's reality. Anyone who does not see the connection does not understand herorhis life in a proper venue from my perspective, which is an opinion, not a force of nature.

I cannot imagine such a situation where one physically dies. The childhood within also dies or is buried. Consciousness continues because it is spiritual as well as physical. One cannot have a lowercase' i' without a dot. The upper case I is a Doric column in my mind, and it is as physical as stone. This stone cannot be seen except through a person's quality of being and herorhis actions taken or not taken in any given circumstance. It is the circumstance that creates the cross and the circle. This is where what is separate in the standard letter is not in the fused in capital letter. Adults were as capital letters in those early days. G-D is a spiritual word. Sometime in my teens, I read G-D spelled with a dash. I leave the alphabet letter out as a symbol of Unknowable. Therefore, G-D is unspellable. That's how I came to understand it. Other people leave the alphabet letter 'o' in or out through their reasoning. I respect that.

Richard: When I was much younger, I stared at one or a small group of lined alphabet letters together, and they moved, barely shuffling. This was likely because no one ever told me that letters and words might move their fixed positions slightly. It was like they were barely waving from time to time, motioning, and perhaps whispering, "Hello, Richard! See me down here. Hi, how are you up there?"

This revelation was an epiphany. It was like discovering that Mommy and I were one, but when I was born, we were two. I had not realized that we were numbers as well as Mommy and Dicky, as I was called then. I quickly learned to answer to my name, which was good because I only spoke coherently in my late twos/early threes. I enjoyed observing and listening and imagining instead.

By observation, Mommy and other family members (father and grandparents) appeared to understand what I needed or wanted. But, of course, all big-sized family members were very good at observation; besides, I was the only kid. That made me unique, and I wanted to be kind to others and pleasant to be with. Mother thought I was most pleasant while playing quietly while she was reading. Since she was reading words and words were my special friends, I didn't mind sharing the time quietly,

Mother told me faery stories when I was three, four, and five; I thought fairies were real beings. It was easy to find them in the front and back yard under leaves or bushes – just a fleeting glimpse then; they darted back to underground nests or into the trunks of trees. Rarely a day when I was outside that I did not take the time to spot a faery or two. I imagined they looked like their pictures in the storybooks. I saw them shuffle about, just like letters and words did.

A couple of those faerie books were Grandma Schick's. Some books looked as old as she did; perhaps the books were even older. Faeries had been around for a long time. Maybe they were as old as the Earth itself. That's what I was told, which became my thought, too, but I never told anyone. Such suppositions stood between the faeries and me alone.

The older word, faeries, is spelled differently than the newer one. Younger faery stories in more recent books spelled the word' fairies.' I observed with my own young eyes and noted the word within, 'air,' was a giveaway. It was a fact and one of mystery, just like the faeries were. The letter shapes were different because of spelling, which made the surrounding empty space different. I imagined the open space. The invisible white space between the words on a horizontal line changed the appearance of the words in a sentence. Were these hidden spaces signs or even secret comments in the shadows even though they were white? I wondered whether 'I' could become an 'E' because of shape-shifting. I kept that secret since I was four or five. Later, I discovered that shape-shifting had a different meaning, but it was still a magical word. I had heard it somewhere, perhaps on an early radio show.

Words were full of mystery and magic, and the pronoun I was just one of those words. Mother told me about pronouns and other parts of speech because I heard adults talking about pronouns and how they were overused and didn't have an Auntie Ceedent.

I understood this as an observable fact about parts of speech like letter combinations on a page. I was in school for several years before I realized Auntie Ceedent was one word, and it was not an aunt like Aunt Ruthie was. I never told anyone lots of things I understood to be true that were not. Another example is one day, I was four years old, and the next day I was five. I still looked and thought the same. What if I had been born at midnight? It seemed adults made arbitrary decisions all the time. I still wonder about the difference between one birthday and the next day. Even today, I still feel the same personality I always was. However, in terms of decades, the difference is quite easily understood after reaching a second decade. It is good that I kept my mouth shut about many things. I made natural misunderstandings. It was no fun discovering I was wrong plenty of times. It is still an excellent reason to shut my mouth and let my fingers talk for Amorella and me.

Amorella: Thank you, Richard. That's it for Chapter One.

OPEN

Chapter Two

In my late seventies, I told my late dear Aunt Ruthie that when I was nearly three, I remember eating mints at a party at Grandma and Grandpa (Mae and Henri) Schick's house at 104 East College Avenue in Westerville, Ohio. She said close friends and family were having a wake for President Franklin Delano Roosevelt, who had recently died in April 1945. I described the east room of the house where family and friends attended the wake.

Aunt Ruthie was surprised, I remembered, but she witnessed the event and collaborated on what and who I had described. I was almost three, I thought FDR was the President's name at the time. His name was accessible because I believed it to be only three letters long. I understood from the elders in the room that he had been a very good man, but I didn't understand what a President was. But then, later in Kindergarten, I realized that Democrats and Republicans existed and that word lengths of both did not make much difference; only the letters did. From then on, I accepted FDR as a nickname as Dick is for Richard.

Later, I learned my other grandfather, Popo, Henri Schick, was a house painter, and a Revenuer for the Ohio Office of Taxation. He worked for the Westerville and Columbus, Ohio Democratic Party. We were few Democrats in a bastion of Republican Westerville in the 1940s. When young, age and appearance in people made differences. A person's appearance was like the shape of each letter, that's how I saw it. People looked similar, either black or white, girls or boys. Girls had longer hair and no penis just like mothers, grandmothers, and

11

aunts, but no one person was a straight or round and ridged as a letter in the alphabet.

This made people more complicated and less likely to compromise on a standard shape and gather in a line or rows of lines; except in parades where soldiers appeared more like letters when they marched in rows. Westerville High School and Otterbein College bands marched in rows too. People who marched together knew what they were doing. Townspeople milling around or shopping did not easily organize or even seem to want to organize together. People shopping followed their own minds, that's what I accepted as valid. Reasoning things out was fun, a game, and it kept me from too much imagination. Mother said I spent too much time in my head and that it wasn't natural for a boy to just sit and think about things. We got along sometimes and sometimes we didn't.

About my fourth year, I discovered that beyond sex and color differentiation, townspeople had come from the same places. No Native Americans lived in the town as far as I knew, but some had lived on Westerville's northwest side, at least according to Popo Orndorff. Most of the white population descended from the British Isles or Europe. The few black people were mainly second, and third-generation freed slaves. People told me these things, but I needed to find out what the British Isles or Europe were, other than homes to ancient faeries and people fighting one another.

One spring day, when I was five, my other grandfather, Popo Orndorff, Clell Tuller Orndorff, lived with my grandmother (Wilhelmina Bookman Orndorff) at 103 West Walnut Street at the southeast corner of Knox Street. I often visited as we lived in a rented double at the southwest corner of Knox and West Park Street. One morning my grandfather introduced me to his neighbor, Mr. Press Reynolds, a very old black man who lived with his wife two or three houses west of my grandparents, on the north side of Walnut Street, across from Otterbein Cemetery. Amorella can tell the story better than I can.

Richard's First Encounter with Mr. Press Reynolds

Amorella . . . Nearly fifty miles east of the bend in the Ohio River, enslaved people crossed to escape slavery by following the Underground Railroad from Kentucky up to the Rankin House at Ripley on the Ohio side. Richard shook hands with a neighbor of his grandparents, Mr. Press Reynolds, who lived on West Walnut Street in Westerville, Ohio. The story is that when Mr. Reynolds was a boy on the plantation, he operated a tobacco press at age ten; thus, he took Press for his first name. It was a Reynolds' plantation, so young Press took Reynolds as his last name. Richard remembers Mr. Reynolds as a kindly old fellow with a workingman's hands. What does it mean to have shaken hands with a man born and raised as an enslaved person, orndorff?

Richard: It was an important event in my life at the time. I was five. I don't remember my thoughts at the meeting other than my grandfather and I were standing on an old side porch, and Mr. Reynolds was standing on the porch with the screen door open. The house paint of the small one-story house was blue. Almost directly across from the house stood, and still stands, the war memorial in the Otterbein College cemetery. Mr. Reynolds was like one of those granite stones that lined the cemetery. As I grew, I learned more about slavery as a matter of course. I mainly remember the event because the man had witnessed the South before the Civil War. I could shake his hand in the present, which would have been 1947.

I had shaken hands with history. At five, I had not thought much about that before, but I gained an early understanding.

13

The cemetery is where I toyed my imagination while walking, running, or sitting among those stones as a child. The concept of generations was something inherently crucial to me and still is. A human generation is something I want to remember when I am dead and physically buried in that same Otterbein Cemetery. I think this is entirely possible because the human spirit and mind are invisible but show themselves anyway, and if anything can survive death, people might.

If there is nothing after death, that's all right too. The natural inclination of the spirit and mind have something to do with it. Perhaps we inwardly fear death enough that we survive it. That would be funny. I feel G-D has a sense of humor, and it might be funny waking up dead. The universe is full of little jokes, and death might be one of them. I thought about these things whenever a great aunt or uncle died. I didn't always go to the funeral but I understood the first significance of being dead was that friends and family would no longer see them alive.

Strangely enough while writing this book, I awoke in the middle of the night with a flash of memory of Mr. Reynolds' boney face and clothed body. He had brightness within his tired eyes, short gray curly hair, and a warm, kind smile for a little one I was when I saw and talked with him in life. I had become one of his friends, and we waved, smiled, and spoke every time we saw one another. He waved again in that flash memory. I saw him wave to me, but I missed hearing his voice. I probably waved back.

Taken from the Orndorff Blog:
Encounters-in-Mind, 19 August 2009

Amorella: *Richard remembers little things that added to his consciousness at age six. First, his father cleans fish caught from Alum Creek: the horror was seeing a bass cut up, and the fish head with large, dark, and dead eyes left on the old nasty stained wood table.*

Richard: Dad always seemed to be fishing or hunting. I never wanted to go along after fishing with him once or twice. Fishing bored me. Why did Daddy always want to be killing things? The cooked fish tasted of a sense of wildness, not pleasant. The idea of killing was repugnant. Dad never killed anyone in World War II, nor was he wounded. Dad did help liberate a concentration camp in 1945. Whenever he got the chance in his long life, Dad fished and hunted. Mom liked to read and listen to music. She was not interested in fishing or hunting either. I remember my parents, eating chips and drinking beer while playing cards with their friends. I would always go to my room to play or nap. I hated the smoke. Mother liked to smoke. Dad chewed cigars down to the stub. Sometimes he chewed the stub until he swallowed it, or when outdoors, he spit it out.

In early grade school, Popo Orndorff took my neighbor friend, Smitty, and me to a Reds' baseball game in Cincinnati. Popo and Grandma also took me out to afternoon dinner on Sundays sometimes. We traveled to several different restaurants within a sixty-mile radius of Westerville. It was fun. With Dad, I would go to Uptown Westerville and watch Dad and his friends play pool. I learned there is another word about hitting a ball or two in a pocket with a long stick. Typically, a pool is where we swim. The name inside the waterless Pool Hall was Billiards. Pool and Billiards, two unlike words that meant almost the same thing. Words could be very confusing, but as usual, I let the mystery go rather than make a fool of myself and ask someone. I hated to ask because nine times out of ten I had to ask the person to repeat it because the words in a line would run away from my ears before I could assimilate them.

Another place Dad, and sometimes Mom, and I would go is up to Auntie and Uncle Doc's hundred-acre plus farm on the south side of Freeman Road, three miles from Uptown. Auntie sometimes carried a gosling in her sweater pocket to keep it warm. She was kind and funny. I liked Uncle Doc because he didn't talk much unless he had something to say. It seemed to me at the time that a lot of people wasted words on what no one wanted to especially hear. I might be wasting some readers' time also, but they can shut the book and read no more of it. I've done that myself from time to time.

Most of those people like Auntie and Uncle Doc are long dead. I know because I went to some of their funerals. Other times, Mom or Dad would just tell me about the funerals. In some ways, funerals were like church and Sunday school because you had to be quiet and behave yourself, so I didn't mind if I didn't have to go. When I didn't go, I usually stayed with someone else in the family that wasn't going. There was an unspoken rule that allowed some family people to stay home and skip the funeral.

I also would visit Auntie and Uncle Doc's dog kennel on the farm, where they raised American cocker spaniels. They had milk cows, straw, mice, birds in the barn, and two large workhorses. I also took time to observe the pigs and the geese. Geese were mean, and I stayed away from them, but I liked the friendlier pigs, ducks, and chickens. Auntie and Uncle Doc had an outhouse, and I would stand or sit and relieve myself – lots of webs, spiders, and bugs scurrying around. Auntie and Uncle Doc lived in an old, story and a half, white-painted house; they had a coal-burning stove in the living room and a big sink in the kitchen and dining table. The second floor had a large bedroom and west window. This was their daughter, Mildred's, room.

When older and married Mildred gave birth to her child in that room. Mildred died of birth complications and shortly after her daughter died also. Auntie and Uncle Doc had only the one child. They never talked about Mildred to me.

They also had an old big black telephone on the wall. You had to call an operator to connect with a neighbor or anyone else. Lots of comfy old furniture and cupboards, some full of interesting colorful doodads and artifacts. They finally earned electricity when I was three or four; so that was mostly the end of kerosene-lit lanterns in the house, by earned I mean they were given electricity by the government but then had to pay for it. Eventually, in the late 40s, the township paved the oil-sprayed gravel Freeman Road, and in 1948, Uncle Doc bought a new gray painted tractor. Grandma Schick was born a Freeman so I supposed the road was named after her family. I remember asking, but I was ignored or misunderstood. Communicating with adult people could be very challenging, and honestly, I found it was not worth the trouble most of the time unless it was my aunts and uncles and grandparents who took time to listen to what I was trying to say. After once or twice on the same subject I my misunderstanding my parents gave up. I don't blame them.

After the war, when I was six, my mother drove me to Washington D.C. to see Father, a soldier who had returned to the States from Europe. There were two-lane roads, and lots of trucks through the Appalachian mountains to the Capitol from Westerville, Ohio. Dad was a Master Sargent stationed south of Washington at Fort Belvoir in Virginia after the war. Then shortly after, he became a second lieutenant. I never understood why at the time, even now, I wonder. I don't know why I didn't ask. I assume I didn't think about it. That was his business anyway, not mine.

Father did not begin as a Master Sargent. In the Fall of 1942, Mother and I lived in an apartment in Juliet, Illinois while Dad worked as a chemist and metallurgist at Joliet Arsenal, a munitions plant near Juliet. In the summer of 1943, Dad transferred to the Manhattan Project, Oak Ridge, Tennessee. Finally, dad was sent to France and Germany in December 1944, just before the Battle of the Bulge. Dad was in the Army Corps of Engineers, and the Army had perfected a steel treadway bridge that the military could quickly put on pneumatic floats for crossing the rivers into Germany. The army they needed those bridges.

Amorella: After the war, there were parades, but what Richard remembers most was the military planes returning to Wright Air Force Base in Dayton.

Richard: As I remember, I was five. Dad rented the first floor of the yellow-painted two-story duplex on the southwest corner of West Park Street and Knox. There was a sidewalk on the south side of West Park down to Westerville Park along Alum Creek and just west of the Otterbein College campus. It was late morning, and I was alone, playing at Westerville Park along Alum Creek, just a short distance from where we lived at 71 West Park Street.

Suddenly, I turned northeast to face an imaginary thirty-degree dark arc of planes in the blue sky. Lines of planes flew overhead, heading southwest toward Wright Air Force Base near Dayton. The constant roar of the bombers' engines shook the ground. The aircraft, primarily bombers, flew at about two thousand feet, or so it seemed, as a vast metal ribbon overhead. This flying-in-formation continued for a half hour or more. I have never before or since viewed so many planes at one time.

In adolescence, I wondered how it would have been to hear those planes dropping bombs. In the 1970s, while teaching in Brazil, I met a student's European Father who had watched such American planes accidentally drop bombs near his farm close to Germany. He and his family were rightfully terrified. I will never forget his story; it was not right for me to mention mine. Early on, I discovered that I am better off listening than talking. However, many of my students over thirty-seven official years would agree that I talked too much; unless, of course, the talking was interrupting a dull lecture. I enjoyed lecturing about authors and their poetry or literature. The conversations were important to students' understandings. Most of the best conversations were spontaneous. I loved it.

Amorella: *Kindergarten was a chore, wasn't it, orndorff?*

Richard: I didn't want to go. We were on Park and Knox, and Kindergarten was in the basement of Emerson, an old elementary school at the time. There were not even fifteen students in the class. I didn't have many social skills with kids my age, partly because I was an only child and there weren't that many kids my age around. I became sullen and angry at having to be in kindergarten even though I secretly liked a few kids, I was too shy to do anything about it. Besides, I was a small kid in the class, a born loner with a terribly secret fear of being misunderstood, and all the muck it caused, me trying to understand what people were talking about, particularly when I asked "why" questions.

My parents and sometimes my grandparents agreed that I could be very thickheaded, sullen and stubborn. Later, I realized people didn't like why questions; they didn't always know the answer. For instance, why do people need to kill other people? I wondered that when I was four and ever since.

19

"Some things are thought out too well, and other things are not thought out well enough." In my eighty-first year that is my response to why people kill one another. I have thought about this for a very, very long time.

Amorella: Richard is debating on putting this in his notebook and not in this book. Why, because he does not like to share all his thoughts. Once he does, they are not his alone. Is this selfish or is it necessary from his perspective? He feels it is necessary. Strange as it may seem, understanding Richard, is from the inside out. His personal opinions/thoughts are all he has. He thinks, 'What's a dead person going to say once sheorhe shares everything in heartansoulanmind? It would all be redundant.'

OPEN

Chapter Three

5 February 2023, Monday

Amorella: You are embarrassed with overusing the I pronoun. You dropped the capital in college as e. e. cummings did with his name and used the standard letter instead.

Richard: I also wrote in the third person, like you, Amorella. I did that in notes, poetry, short stories, and novels. I am more detached and objective in the third person.

The style of writing I use in this book would be more straightforward if it were in a regular, old-fashioned, dated journal format from the eighteenth century, like the journals of literary heroes such as Johnathon Swift or Voltaire. This book aims to reach people interested in a hypothetical or theoretical environment.

Amorella: Mr. Orndorff appears to forget that I, the Amorella, suggested he allow me to direct the nature of this work.

Richard: Yes, this work is written because Amorella feels that giving an added perspective to life is essential. The psychological sense of a person's surviving heartansoulanmind after physical death is critical. I am still a spiritually oriented person, and I am not dead yet. I enjoy writing.

Amorella: Richard is more unique in his open honesty than he feels, enough so for me to be here writing through his fingertips.

This third chapter shows two more important pre-school events. The first is about Dickie, as he was called, taking imaginary coins from his bedroom wall to buy a chocolate milkshake at Dews Drug Store, a block away, Uptown.

Richard: I was four or five and hungry for a milkshake. Mother was not ready to go to Dews. The doctor said I was too skinny and needed to gain weight, which was the reason for the milkshakes in the first place. The time was late morning in Spring. Dews was on the west side of State Street, across from Williams Grill. The Greyhound Bus Stop going north was at Williams Grill. The bus stop going south was at Dews across on the west side of State Street, a much smaller eatery with a white marble counter serving area, dark brown booths, and many drug store-type items. Both restaurants sold ice cream, sodas, sandwiches, daily newspapers, and a wide variety of weekly magazines for bus travelers going near or far in either direction.

I like Dews better. I began pulling ten pennies from the wall in my bedroom, and I put them in my pocket. I told Mother I was leaving for Dews, and she asked where I got the money. I replied, "From my wall savings." She met me at the door and asked to see the money. I didn't want to show her, so we walked to my room,

Mother politely asked, "Which wall?"

I pointed.

She said, "There are no pennies on the wall.

I replied, "I have them in my pocket."

She sarcastically commented, "Show them to me."

I had no coins in my pocket, but I remembered pulling them from the wall after I had placed the pennies in three lines of ten on the wall the day before. Mother grew quietly anxious when I wondered aloud where the other two lines of ten pennies were and the ones I had put in my pocket. I had only taken ten off the wall. Mother wondered how and why I stuck the pennies on the wall in the first place, and asked "Where they were?" I shrugged my shoulders and said I didn't know.

Later, we went Uptown to Dews in mid-afternoon after she had made a grilled cheese sandwich and purple grapes on the side for my lunch. That evening, Mother and Father argued about my ability to separate imagination from reality. They wanted me to see a particular doctor, and I didn't. I told them I would not put more pennies on the wall, and that was that.

I realized I could think these things out for myself. If I kept quiet Mother or Father couldn't ask me silly questions that I had no responses for. I remember silently whispering to myself, 'imagination is not a reality, it sometimes feels so. It is a word. After all, feelings are real even if imagination is not. My words come from imagination and thinking, and term words, as Mother called them exist in grammar. Mom and Dad needed to think more clearly. I learned early on how to put up with my inquisitive parents. Term words were real words like wall and chair. Other words were what I called add-ons so I didn't mix nouns and verbs up with walls and chairs. These matters were quite difficult for me at the time.

Amorella: What else did you learn in those days, orndorff?

the St. Louis Cardinals. I never knew why he turned it down. He loved softball and baseball. I didn't ask why he turned it down. Now that I am eighty-one, it suddenly feels important. There was no reason not to question Uncle Ernie about it in all those years I knew him, but I didn't.

By the time I was four or five I went to Sunday School at our local First Presbyterian Church on the corners of Knox Street and West College Avenue, I learned about Jesus. One time, Jesus' disciples were on a boat in the Sea of Galilee witnessing Jesus' walking towards them on the Sea of Galilee. We even saw a picture of an old painting depicting this scene in Sunday School class. At first, like the other children, I accepted this as a fact, but a little later, while thinking about this, the story didn't seem right. Why? Jesus was the Son of God. He looked like everyone else, so I assumed we were all God's children. I didn't tell anyone what I thought because I knew better. Mother always politely said, "It is best that you not to talk too much because people sometimes misunderstand your responses to their questions."

Mother was right, that's the way it was. People needed to understand I needed to get the parts of speech in the proper order by listening closely. Sometimes I didn't understand why they put their words together without seemingly to think first. People would pause, or change the subject, or use words I didn't know or understand, or words I understood all too well such as, "Why aren't you paying attention?" or "Don't you hear or understand what I am saying?"

It was a Sunday afternoon in late Spring, 1945, and I was standing with Mother on a dock on a small island with canoe storage racks just north of the Alum Creek bridge on Main Street. As I stood at the end of the dock, fully dressed in shorts, a shirt and shoes, I jumped in and sank like a rock. Mother knew I could swim and saw me as I came up. She asked with caution, "Why did you jump in the water, fully dressed?" In shock and without a thought, I mumbled with a straight face, "Well, Jesus could walk on water, so I thought I might too."

Mother was peeved with me for having said, *"jump in,"* when I was trying *to walk on* and didn't know what to say, so she politely smiled and commented, "Let's go home, change into some dry clothes, then we can come back." After that, we never discussed this incident again. However, this event quickly reinforced my realization of why I need to keep my thoughts private. I was attempting to walk on and sank like a rock. That's the truth of it. All I could think of at the time was, "Why didn't people try to walk on water like Jesus?" Nobody ever did as far as I knew. These were the kind of simple yet confusing incidents that happened at least once a month. I would try something because nobody informed me not to. I could accept, "Don't cross the road without looking." I remember thinking, why would I not look? As I grew older, I changed this in my mind to: "Don't cross the road without thinking," not looking because one has to think something first before doing it. I thought it strange.

Sometimes though Grandma, either one, would say, "Remember to look before crossing." That made more sense and I usually smiled at the comment, no matter who said it. If someone asked why I was smiling I would say, "Nothing." People didn't always take kindly to me saying, "Nothing" because they thought I was too smart for my britches. That comment never made any sense to me. How could I be too smart for my pants? I never responded, but once I did, and whoever it was looked at

Chapter Four

10 February 2023, Friday

Amorella: Richard finished the first and one or two months of the second grades at Longfellow Elementary at the northeast corner of Know Street and Hiawatha Avenue in Westerville. At the same time, he lived with his grandparents, parents, and little sister on the southeast corner of Knox and Walnut, about two blocks north. In late September, Red Noble finished the two-story house on Minerva Lake Road in Minerva Park. The white-painted house had contrasted dark green window shutters and a dark green roof on the street side only. Uptown Westerville is about three miles north of our home. About a mile west is the brick two-story Minerva Park Elementary on Cleveland Avenue, built in 1924 and eventually bought by the Westerville Board of Education. Hawthorne Elementary replaced Minerva Park in the late 1950s.

Richard: Moving into the Minerva Lake Road house with all the new aromas, mainly wood and paint, was a shock. The basement was dry, or it appeared to be. I had rarely visited a dry basement my whole life; most of those walls were damp, and cement floors were known to draw up water. We had a working toilet in the northwest corner of the basement next to the washer and dryer. Dad eventually hooked up some wire near the ceiling and hung a mostly solid brown bathtub shower curtain around it for privacy. In the early days, the basement was for storage. After heavy rain, some wetness oozed from where the concrete wall blocks connected with the damp concrete. I found it an exciting place to hang out because no one wanted to be there. We put in a couple of old stuffed chairs and old floor lamps. I particularly enjoyed walking barefoot on the dry concrete floor in the summer.

Amorella: Second grade was a learning experience, primarily social learning, what was acceptable on the playground and what was not. The third grade was much the same, particularly with schoolwork. The third grade was the last year Richard enjoyed school with overall As and a B or two in his subjects. The playground experience was almost always relaxing and fun. Summers were chiefly spent at the two Minerva lakes. One to the north of Minerva Lake Road and one to the south. The north side has about four feet of grass and trees before touching the water; the south has eight feet of grass and vegetation before the lake's touch. The naturally appropriate bushes and trees surrounding the lakes set the mood for kids to explore beyond the road.

Richard: I enjoyed my Westerville school years also. The social aspect of growing with friends and maturing through our teens. My third-grade teacher, the young, pretty, and caring Mrs. Munger. I would have done anything she asked and did. Once, while at her desk, she politely asked me if I would participate in the Christmas program. The invitation was given so I could turn it down. I had no desire to be on stage alone or with others. However, Mrs. M's sweet angelic- eyes whispered a *please, so* I said I would.

I mentioned I couldn't carry a tune (that's what Mom always told me), which Mrs. M. also understood. I stood behind the bell on the stage, moving it from side to side. I didn't have to sing; I mouthed the words for those who could see me. Mrs. M. was very kind. I will never forget her as a personal, professional, and energetic personality. I had never had a teacher so young and vibrant before.

In elementary school, most of the teachers were older women. They were also kind, like both of my grandmothers. Some teachers were better liked than others. We, children, knew to be polite and respect our elders long before entering a classroom. We understood and accepted this by the third grade as a part of G-D's sense of dark humor. Sometimes, while lying in bed trying to sleep, I thought about G-D and how, in the Holy Bible, G-D decided, through Moses, what the sins were. I assumed G-D also understood what accidents or misjudgments were.

This was a private assumption, hoping G-D would declare me an accidental birth because I was not necessarily a wanted child. At least, that was what I concluded, even though Mother was kind and patient with me most of the time. My misunderstanding of how the world was, is my problem, not hers. Some events appear to have no purpose. Since this is the case, why would I conclude I have a sense of purpose? People suppose they have a sense of purpose, and if they don't have one, they make one up. Well, I don't really know about other people, in that way, even friends and family. It seems to me that from Kindergarten on through college I was making up what I wanted to be. And, then, in my forties and fifties, I wondered what I wanted to be until somewhere in my seventies, then I was content until I realized the only thing I knew how to do was read and write, so I decided to try to write better by more deeply assessing who I was in heartansoulanmind.

Early on, I became interested in G-D because of Jesus and Sunday school at the Westerville First Presbyterian Church. I did not understand why Jesus was so important when His Father was an Absolute G-D. I felt good about my ability to observe my peers objectively, parents, teachers, and even Jesus because he had been a person. Jesus, the person, was an accepted fact of nature to me. I slowly became conscious of a Spirit of G-D, especially when I was still, silent, and alone in thought.

I recognize how I view G-D as metaphysical. It is not the same as 'sensing' someone else is in the room when I am alone, nor is it the same as 'sensing' a lesser spirit is in the room. My sense of G-D in the room is when I suddenly in the impending Quiet, I feel clothed with humility rather than goosebumps. Perhaps this is a built-in safety precaution within my spirituality and my heartansoulanmind, when I think I am less than Nothing. This is my thought brings out my personal metaphysics, which is, Understanding I am less than Nothing.

Amorella: What Richard means to say is, "Within G-D's Presence, I feel I am Nothing."

Richard: In 1951, I was unsettled in the fourth grade at Minerva Park School. First, I had Mrs. Spence., who was quite a bit older than Mrs. Munger. She appeared to have a no-nonsense demeanor. I didn't mind the learning in her class, except I had trouble understanding fractions. My interests also leaned toward social and athletic events. I still liked stories, history, and science.

Amorella: By Spring 1952, Little League baseball had more fully developed in the Westerville community. Richard was a part of one of the four original teams, the Supermen.

Richard: I remember being excited about making the team, and after some work, I was selected to be one of the pitchers, but I found I had problems almost immediately. The home plate moved when I attempted to throw the baseball over it. After explaining this to the coach, I took an eye examination and was told I needed eyeglasses because, at ten years old, I had nearsightedness and stigmatism. Glasses certainly helped my pitching abilities, but having eyeglasses helped me recognize that as a kid, when I had seen faeries in the shrubberies and near tree trunks it was because stigmatism allowed me to better 'imagine' rocks and other small inanimate objects appearing alive. After all, they shuffle on their own before me having glasses.

Knowing I had stigmatism allowed me to realize some of my early childhood observations were false, and it wasn't because of my imagination. Stigmatism is a reality. This event made me want to question physical validity more profoundly. It helped broaden my aspects of fantasy and reality. Non-living things moved because my brain said they did. My eyes and brain did not function normally.

Having eyeglasses fixed the problem. Science solved my issues, just as it had my premature birth. Science became a personal revelation, and knowledgeable, scientifically minded people became crucial in a deeper part of my private life. Science mostly replaced childish wonders such as faeries and the like. Acquiring personal knowledge created a more secure psychological environment.

Amorella: By fourth grade, you had two main boyfriends: Don and Doug. They both lived south of Minerva Park off the east side of Cleveland Avenue, within a quarter mile of Herder's Market, a place you would ride your bike to for candy bars and soft drinks. Your other two friends were girls, Susan and Sandy. They lived in Minerva Park, and you visited both periodically when you rode your bike from school, and you would stop and talk to them after they got home on the bus.

Richard: Don was good sized and athletic, and you got to know him on the playground. He also had an exciting family. His father worked in home construction. He had a bulldozer and all the surrounding equipment. Donnie had several brothers; his mother was a wonderful lady who put up with four boys and the father. His mother had a player piano, and his father had a 1938 Cord automobile, among others. I used to love to listen to that player's piano, and sometimes, when invited, I would sit and eat lunch with them on a Saturday or in the summer, anytime I was there, and lunch was being served. I loved the bread, baked beans, and hot dogs – mustard, ketchup, relish, onion, and potato chips. I loved the fellowship. Donnie's mother was a saint.

Doug was athletic too, but smaller-boned than Don, and he was more earnest in his studies. We usually talked about science and history. We like both. Doug's father was in business, but he was always interested in science projects at home. When we were older, I remember he built a refractile telescope by hand. He polished the lenses himself. The man had tremendous and exacting patience on his projects. Doug's mother was also a saint like Don's mother. Like Donnie's mother, Doug's mother was friendly and patient with her family and with me. Doug also had two younger brothers and a sister. I would have given anything to have been adopted by either the Landis or the Goss family. Such comradery. My relationship with Mother and Father waned. Everyone in our family was busy but not always busy together. Each of us grew a separate family life.

My friends who were girls, Susan and Sandy, lived about five houses from each other on Wildwood. Susan was closer to Cleveland Avenue and the school. Mostly, we rode our bikes and chatted about school and the teachers and students, as well as about the other kids who lived close by in Minerva Park. We knew each other from the third grade. They were fun to talk to and, as friends, helped reassure me that it was okay to like girls at that upper elementary level. Tabitha, who was already friends with Susan and Sandy, lived closer to me on Minerva Lake Road, was also a friend. [I just saw Tabitha a few weeks ago, October, 2023, the first time since graduation, and it was a wonderful for both of us.] Then, in the fifth grade, I recently gained a second sister, Gretchen. I was ten. Cathy was five.

Gretchen was born in early April 1952. It is easy to remember because Mom and Dad were at the hospital, and I was down on the north side of Rt. 161, west of Cleveland Avenue, shooting rats at the corn storage units behind the house of another friend, Rodney. Rodney's father, Mr. Troutman was our scoutmaster, a kind, patient man. I like him a lot. It was sad when he died suddenly. Mr. Andrews who lived in Westerville became our scoutmaster. I loved scouting. We used to go on trips and campouts, sometimes at Auntie and Uncle Docs on Freeman Road.

Dad was interested in my scouting experiences because he became an Eagle Scout in high school. Dad became our assistant scoutmaster; he and Mr. Andrews, the scoutmaster. They were friends. I was supposed to take Dad's Eagle Scout experiences as a challenge, but I never did. When in high school and a scout Explorer, I earned a Star rank while an eighth or ninth grader and was working on Life Scout rank when I quit as a tenth grader. Father never said a thing, but I'm sure he was disappointed I couldn't muster up. I didn't care one bit. Ever-changing public high school experiences proved to be much more enjoyable than scouting.

Richard: Preadolescence began with a dribble of semen in the sixth grade. I understood the concept but not the reality of discovering the dribble once every week or so on my sleeping

OPEN

Chapter Five

17 February 2023, Thursday

Richard: Emerson Junior High (originally Vine Street School) is a brick building two stories high with a full basement that had windows half way up the walls. Janitorial services and furnace and storage were located. With windowed turrets on the north and south sides, it still looks like a castle. The building faces west along Vine Street and is four to five feet up from the sidewalk. The school opened in the Spring, 1896. Originally, students brought their lunch or went home when Grandma Orndorff. entered in the third grade, nor was there electricity or toilets within the school. Grandma also saw electricity installed in 1914, and she graduated from Vine Street School in 1916, the same year Kindergarten was added. In 1954, when our class entered seventh grade. Kindergarten was in the basement which had a south side entrance. The playground is on the east side of the building not too far from the railroad track, the train station, and the Westerville Creamery and southside behind Grandpa and Grandma Schick's house and others on the north side of East College Avenue two blocks east of State Street.

Amorella: The excitement of entering Emerson Junior High pressed through Richard's arteries. He was becoming adolescent and understanding his place in the world by reading the Orndorff Family history through the research of his Great Aunt Floy as well as Ohio history, and dabbling through the <u>World Encyclopedia;</u> and his mother's signed (Mary Laverna Schick) on the inside of her red-covered, Bartlett's <u>Famous Quotations,</u> 11th edition, 1941.

Amorella: You appear to be honest, orndorff, but you just don't give a damn whether I'm an Angel or not?

Richard: I don't believe in Angels, per se, but in deep spiritual memory, I wonder on Michael and Satan. I had a Presbyterian upbring. I can't help that it is still in my mind.

Amorella: You just referred to Michael and Satan, not Jesus and Satan.

Richard: I did? I must be thinking of Milton's *Paradise Lost* not the *Bible*. Michael does defeats Satan in Book XI and XII where Adam and Eve exist.

Amorella: You are in the Place of the Dead and debating Milton and the Bible?

Richard: I wondered if you were going to put a question at the end of the statement.

Amorella. You wondered on the question because you forget you are dead. This happens with the newly dead. The main question for you, orndorff, is what you are going to do now in this newly 'natural' human setting?

Richard: I cared about things my entire life. My life was full of worry, apprehension, and worst of all, a dark imagination. Hauntings of Steve's up-front question on entering high school, "Cheer up things are bound to get worse."

Amorella: *Life can't get any worse, or any better for you, orndorff. You are dead.* - Amorella

Richard: That doesn't sound very angelic-like, Amorella.

Amorella: *Who are you to know what an Angel is like?*

Richard: I don't feel hopeful knowing either.

Amorella: *Why should you feel hopeful? Besides, thinking on the constructions of angels, remember when your daughter, Kim, took that junior trip to Paris with French class?*

Richard: Yes, I do. She was so excited. Her mother, Carol, had been to France. I had never been. Except once when old friends Alta and Craig and Carol and I traveled through parts of Italy, and the plane we took from Rome landed at Charles de Gaulle Airport in Paris on the way home. I can't remember whether we got out of the plane in Paris or not. I think we did because we had to transfer to an American airline.

Amorella: *Does it make any difference now that you are dead?*

Richard: No. Anyway, Kim and her French teacher, Mrs. Gwen Good, and friends went to the bookstore, Shakespeare, and Company, in the Fall of 1995. The famous quotation on angels hangs written above the doorway of the reading room: **"Be not inhospitable to strangers lest they be angels in disguise."** I always put this quotation on the board while teaching early

20th century English Literature: sometimes I did earlier, when teaching *Paradise Lost*.

[**Aside.** This is Orndorff. On Wednesday afternoon of 15 February 2023. I called Kim to check the information above, and as I mentioned "Shakespeare, and Company." Kim quieted, politely stopped me from talking, and clearly said, "Be not inhospitable to strangers lest they be angels in disguise." She also noted that I put the quote on the board several times during AP English her senior year. Kim was as proud in remembering as I am proud for not only for her remembering the quotation, but, more importantly, with the energy and excitement, our 43-year-old daughter repeated the words to me. That energy and excitement might just as well still be in my AP Literature class. What a wonderful daughter Carol and I have. Kim Orndorff-Paik is one of those angels in disguise as far as I am concerned.]

Amorella. *You bring such memories with you, Richard. This is an excellent example of being in the newly dead spiritual experience. One is never free of being a human spirit.*

Richard: I had not thought that. This shows, to me, a perception of Reality I have not glimpsed. Where are you going, Amorella?

Amorella: *I am recollecting your thoughts on the spiritual event in joining the Presbyterian Church in 1955.*

Richard: A few days before joining the church we had a meeting with the pastor, a reminder of what we had studied. This focused our accepting the Apostles' Creed (KJV). At the age of twelve I accepted this:

Apostles' Creed (KJV)

I believe in God, the Father almighty, Creator of heaven and earth, and in Jesus Christ, his only Son, our Lord, and in Jesus Christ, his only Son, our Lord, who was conceived by the Holy Spirit, born of the Virgin Mary, suffered under Pontius Pilate, was crucified, died, and was buried; [----] he ascended into heaven, and is seated at the right hand of God the Father almighty; from there he will come to judge the quick and the dead. I believe in the Holy Spirit, the holy catholic* Church the communion of saints, the forgiveness of sins, the resurrection of the body, and life everlasting. Amen.

I did not accept:

". . . he descended into hell; on the third day he
rose again from the dead; . . .."

I also, had trouble with the line: ". . . and is seated at the right hand of God . . ." because I did not know if God had a right hand or a left either, but I accepted it figuratively; "descending into hell;" sounds literal to me, particularly with the added, "third day".

In any case, on a following Sunday morning we had to repeat the Apostle's Creed with the assumption by the pastor and congregation that we believed it. I was taught to be honest and polite. I could not think of a polite way to interrupt the proceedings and explain why I didn't believe fully in what was written and what I was going to say. Here I was; dishonest in front of my peers, the pastor, and the rest of the congregation; in church no less. I was literally dishonest in church. Ever after that, when I attended any church for whatever reason my faith crumbled a bit more.

Amorella: I accept this as an honest account from your heartansoulanmind.

Richard: I have since concluded, in my last few years, that G-D exists, through observation, reason and understanding. I accept G-D exists based (within the context of utmost humility) on my judgment from heartansoulanmind. Like Martin Luther, translated of course, "I can do no other."

I, the Amorella, also accept this as an honest statement from within your heartansoulanmind.

Richard: Another event comes to mind. In the eighth grade I had Mr. O'Connell for math. We did not get along because I dreaded any subject in which I had no confidence. At the end of class and before the bell rang to proceed to the next Mr. O'Connell caught me with a piece of pornography a fellow classmate had just passed to me.

As I took a quick shocking glance, the teacher caught me and quickly took the photograph, the first pornography I had ever seen. I could not think of anything to say except, "Billy just handed it to me," as the bell rang.

Mr. O'Connell kept us both while staring sternly. I don't think Mr. O'Connell knew what to say either. People were coming into class. All I could think was 'Detention' with a note home for parental signing as to the infraction. He dismissed us, saying he would speak to the principal on the matter. The dark shade of dread smothered me into the next week.

Eventually, the principal stopped me in the hall saying I had a detention. He did not mention whether he contacted my parents. Dread lingered for the rest of the week but nothing was ever said at home. I was horrified from the moment I was caught through the rest of junior high school. I said nothing to anyone. When I thought on the incident, I prayed to G-D, "Please do not let anyone else find out about this. Thank you." Occasionally, after saying this silent prayer, I heard a voice say (though not the quiet cadence of yours Amorella), "You muddied your own water, Boy." I stopped the praying.

This is the lesson I learned. Don't bother G-D or anyone else over tra-la-la, shit.

Amorella: You capitalized, 'Boy' as in "You muddied your own water, Boy,"

Richard: I have trouble overthinking capitalization or anything else.

Amorella: Really?

Richard: One thing I don't have to overthink are long time friendships. Doug is my oldest male friend. We relate on a variety of levels, one of those levels is philosophical bordering on metaphysical. We are still genuinely interested in what spiritual life is after death. My second oldest male friend is Fritz, we are also interested in philosophy and government. Both friends focused on logic, reason, and intuition. In fact, I don't believe I have ever had a close friend who did not drill into logic, reason, observation, philosophy, and intuition while problem-solving. Doug (John in high school) majored in nuclear physics. Fritz majored in law. Other friends have been college or high school teachers. I do not remember a friend, male or female, who was not a reader.

Amorella. This is a review of your life, orndorff, not your friends.

Richard. I cannot separate my friends from my life, Amorella. I would not be who I am without my close friends some of whom, I'm sad to say, are deader than I am presently. Will I see my friends and family in this spiritual life, Amorella?

Amorella: You recognize you have a spiritual memory, which is more precise and exact than biological memory. Your subconscious wills a fuller memory, particularly when it comes to family and/or close friends. The pattern remembered is also in context with given situations, otherwise, why would any memory exist. For instance, not long ago you asked Fritz about how things were in junior high school – what did you remember being important?

Fritz could not offer anything substantial about the eighth grade other than he was the editor of the junior high newspaper which was runoff on the mimeograph machine. He does remember going on a trip or two in Ohio History and that you were along, but he doesn't remember you both riding in the same car.

Richard: Fritz was one of my new friends in the eighth grade when he and several of his classmates from the seventh grade transferred from the nearby Blendon Township School when it incorporated with Westerville public schools. I had Mrs. Needham for English, Mrs. Caldwell for Reading, Mr. Franklin for Geography, Mr. Morgan for Science, and Mr. O'Connell for Mathematics. Most everyone had at two or three of those teachers in the eighth grade.

In junior high my friends and I lost Phillip Crane, one of our own since the fifth grade. Phillip died in an automobile accident while on a family trip to northwestern Ohio. It was uncommonly sad for many of us had not yet lost a friend from a death. I have never forgotten where he is buried at Otterbein Cemetery; he is buried to the northeast of me, less than two hundred or so feet from me.

Amorella. *Your spirit nor anyone else's spirit is buried anywhere, orndorff.*

Richard: How is this, Amorella, that you still call me Orndorff, the name etched in the shared headstone of my wife, Carol, and me?

Amorella: *This is your name until you rename yourself with the few words that best describe who you were when you died.*

Richard: I don't like this one bit.

Amorella: *Why is this?*

Richard: I didn't ask to be renamed.

Amorella: You didn't ask to be named when you were born either. This is an exercise, orndorff, like an assignment.

Richard: What if I don't do it, Amorella. I have free will.

Amorella. You will not be able to find your friends and family, and they will not be able to find you. This your choice, of course.

Richard: Can I change my mind?

Amorella: "ay there's the rub: for in that sleep of death what dreams may come?"

Richard: One has problems when alive, and it seems there are more problems when dead.

Amorella: *Fewer problems, not more, Mr. Orndorff.*

- A Background and Transition -

Amorella: Richard's Guardian Spirit, here. The dimension I am from is Nothing but with a capital N. Now, a little background about Guardian Spirits.

Once physically dead, **human hearts** *occasionally embrace without their souls attached. Those who embrace may disappear from the Place of the Dead, never to be recognized again. I, Amorella, know two such human hearts. We call them* **Humanella**.

Amorella: I am reminding you, orndorff, you awoke in the night, lumbered into the dark living room, and clicked on the switch to the fire in the fireplace. Sitting quietly in the brown lounger, you watched the flickering of a real flame without accompanying natural wood – no cracking of downed damp tree limbs, no scented wood smells, either – it seems a harsh setting. Purgatory, comes to your mind. In this setting, a forgotten memory is vividly recalled. Purgatory vanishes.

Richard: I just remembered to include a significant fun moment of junior high. It was a Saturday night, though the date was unimportant. My taller girlfriend, Kay, and I won a dance trophy in the basement of the Presbyterian Church at the corner of Knox and College in Uptown Westerville. I had forgotten about it, but in the love and kindness of a special relationship, Kay showed me the small gold-painted trophy at our 50th Year high school reunion.

The last time I saw Kay was before our graduation in 1960. The last time I saw the award was in 1955. Kay had saved the trophy as a reminder of a fun time. We did have fun at those basement dances, but it was in her remembrance. A quiet and private thought flashed from my heart to my soul. We are still kindred spirits from a timeless place in that small, seemingly unimportant event now re-membered while dead. Such a gesture of love and kindness in friendship is not spiritually forgotten.

Amorella: The above shows the truth of how it is being dead. Not so well described as Richard had hoped, but real enough in heartansoulanmind. A small, seemingly unimportant act of sharing after all those years becomes so much more important because it hints at what life was and is while transitioning from physical death into spiritual consciousness. This example serves as a sacred yet, simple friendship memory with no intent other than simply sharing. This is how messages are sent and received from one raised heart to another. Simply sharing.

Richard: I am left speechless in gratitude for this kind, loving, shared thought.

Amorella: *You are as dead; and still speechless, orndorff. – Amorella*

Amorella: *Now, if the Reader so wills, sheorhe may continue on to Chapter Six. Thank you.*

OPEN

Chapter Six

Richard: It is summer in 1956 and I am swimming at Glengarry Pool, a couple miles south of Minerva Park and a mile or two north of Westerville on Westerville Road (State Route 3). This is a fun time before my soon to be Freshman year. Doug and I both built model airplanes and cars this summer. Doug also takes me on his used Cushman motor scooter to various places of shared interests. Listening to short-wave radio and tinkering with discarded radios and TVs was another summer/fall hobby. A neighbor, a veteran by the name of Allen, learned about the radio business in the U. S. Army. He fixes radios and televisions for people, charging little more than what it cost for parts. I like to talk radio with him because I always could learn something free of charge. Nice fellow. I wish I could remember his first name.

Amorella: Other outside interests were astronomy and science fiction. Bike riding, taking the fishing boat to Minerva Lake South, and collecting Boy Scout merit badges. Music: country, bluegrass, blues, rock, folk, Medieval folk, and Latin chant choirs. And sixteenth through twentieth centuries; famous symphonies, and added musicals of the late nineteenth and twentieth centuries were Richard's interests and pleasures.

Richard: Suddenly, it was the first morning of Fall classes at Westerville High School. I was anxious because it was a new environment, and I would meet scheduled teachers to find out which friends were in each of my classes. The freshman classes were English, Social Studies, Latin I, Natural Sciences, Algebra

I, Football. The sophomore year would be like Geometry rather than Algebra I, and required World History.

I watched the Cleveland Browns on Sunday during their season and went to Ohio State home football games, where I ushered in the south stadium bleachers as a Boy Scout Explorer. I had a passion for what I've been reminiscing, but I needed more enthusiasm to be sustainable all the time.

Amorella: You were thinking of the opening day of Freshman year. You got off the bus on State Street facing the school. Walking towards the front doors, you meet up with your friend Steve and about ten feet in front of the school doors, Steve Gardner turns to you and in his usual deadpan fashion, says with a slight grin, "Cheer up; things are bound to get worse."

Richard: I will never forget that moment and those classically cadenced dark-humored words.

Amorella: Apparently so.

Richard: Upon getting off Bus 8, I first saw my second cousin, Charlene Short. She waved friendly on the way to school. She was a senior, and her younger brother, David, was in the eighth grade. We got along okay. Grandpa Orndorff's oldest sister was named Gretchen. He had five older sisters. Gretchen was Charlene and David's Grandmother on the Orndorff side. Mr. Robert Short, their father, taught math classes primarily to upperclassmen, as we called them in those days. I dreaded the day I would have him for a math class. I quietly asked G-D to spare us both the trouble. I was most apprehensive about math, not the teacher, a good old fellow who had fought in the war. Once through the high school doors, Steve and I walked up the marbled stairs to the first floor and began looking for our homeroom postings near our lockers. That's all I remember. Some of us were taller than in the Spring. The teachers, other than coaches, were mainly new to us.

By the end of the school day, my anxiety greatly lessened. Steve might have been wrong with his predictive statement at the school entrance. Familiar faces in the hall and classrooms had put me at ease. Then while we were leaving for the buses, I saw a couple oversized sophomore boys checking us out with deliberately mean looks. I remember looking down, trying to avoid them.

Thinking back, I should have presented myself more forcefully. I was on the Freshman football team, but my timidity and basic shyness showed through my face and body. I knew this; I felt the storm clouds in my head but thought I could do nothing about it at the time. Besides, I didn't want to get beat up after school on the first day. On the bus home, I thought about how Steve was right. Things were bound to get worse. Arriving home, I realized that Algebra I and Latin I were huge boulders I would either learn to climb or be crushed by.

Amorella: Orndorff's feelings above are true to form. The 'sense' of his day touches on the various moods in and out of the hallways. Feelings can be mistakenly taken as facts, especially in adolescence. Not remembering everything precisely as it was is common among human beings, which can be in a twenty-four-hour period or nearly seventy years ago. Many may not even recognize how long they have been dead when working these memory matters out for themselves. Time has a way of slipping away when one is focused on critical personal projects, and that's with human beings among the living. Imagine, if you will, how it is being dead, where time will never return. Being recently deceased takes a focus, you see, not generally realized while alive.

Being dead can be intimating and humbling, too. Don't you think, orndorff?

Richard: Wow, Amorella. I had to reread this to realize what the words imply. I would not have thought to express this on my own. I am humbled. I tell you, this being dead is an awkward and strange feeling. I'm just not in the world anymore.

Amorella: *Indeed, it is a new feeling, orndorff, I'll grant you that. You aren't even entirely dead, so to speak. Or, it's just your imagination in play. This new feeling you have would scare some people, but you are not afraid or even that intimated by me. You are eighty years old and don't give a damn. I like your sense of humor, old man, it's as dark as ever.*

Richard: This is a twist I have not seen lately. You are funny, Amorella. You have a great sense of humor. I am glad you are my Guardian Spirit in this Journal. You are making me feel very much more at ease. Thank you for your kindness and for this sudden flush of humility.

Amorella: *Doug, Fritz, and Steve are three of your closest old friends of those days in heartansoulanmind. You still confided in all three. The problem is defining the term, **friend**, among the living and the dead. **Readers;** here is what I find in the New Oxford Dictionary on orndorff's laptop:*

ORIGIN Old English frēond, of Germanic origin; related to Dutch vriend and German Freund, from an Indo-European root meaning 'to love,' shared by free.

Amorella: The Reader can see the closest friends are loved most deeply through sharing themselves; in this book, a friend is one with whom one can more easily share the whole of herorhis heartansoulanmind in life. In this work, these are the 'friends' one may most likely first visit after physical death. Among the dead I visit in this work, 'friends and family' may be considered the same with most.

Richard: I am impressed with how simply you put this, Amorella.

Amorella: Conscious friendship after physical death meets simpler and yet more profound individual guidelines.

Richard: I need to focus on my closer friends, those friends I see more regularly in those high school years. Friends in the Class of 1960. I ran around with these friends during all four years: Mary Ann Arthur, Jerry Beaver, Ken Crouch, Jo Elberfeld, Charlie Ferguson, Steve Gardner, John Douglas Goss, Ann Griffith, Kay Griffith, Sandy Hennacy, Gary Jackson, Scharry Jones, Tom Kahler, Judy Krebs, Don Landis, Donna Lust, George Miles, Bill Miller, Fritz Milligan, George Musson, Jean Noble, Dale Patterson, Carol Pfeager, Barbra Popovich, Barb Renner, Judy Scarfpin, Donna Schneider, Bill Shackson, Beverly Steele, Shirley Thomas, Rod Troutman, Richard Vance, Jack Weisenstein, Ron Wilke, Bill Wilkin, Sandy Williams, Tabitha Williams, Steve Wood, and Bill Wren. These were people in most of my classes and/or activities at one time or another during all four years.

Amorella: You need help selecting stronger Oxford' Old English' defined friendships. I am providing the individuals who cut more profoundly into your heartansoulanmind during high school by adding an underline.

Richard: In studying the list, I could intuitively sense the reason(s) why each is underlined and agree wholeheartedly. The others I still consider friends. And I had a few friends from the Classes of 1961. So, I add Craig Brelsford, Bob Clawson, Tom Fletcher, Bob Pringle, Louie Steinmetz, David Short, Ron Bott, and Jane Scott.

Amorella: I underlined above, those who fit your heart's friendship criteria.

Richard: Strangely, I agree wholeheartedly. The others were good friends also, but not for my lifetime.

Amorella: You have a loss for words to explain your recognized and underlined friendships. Here is your problem as I, the Amorella, see it. Friendships are built into one's humanity through one's heartansoulanmind. The heart and mind struggle with choosing words with significance. Love is not the right word because it is overused. Attraction is a lesser word than affection, yet in this work's context, "an indiscernible endearment" is a significantly better way to express a deep, lasting friendship. You may disagree, orndorff. I am only making this a personal point to you. I observe its immediate effectiveness.

Richard: It is. Indeed, you are as a Guardian Spirit. Friendship is an indiscernible endearment. This sounds like something my late Aunt Ruthie might whisper to me from beyond the grave. This thought is so unexpected?

Amorella: This realization is expected, orndorff.

Richard: What a special surprise you and Aunt Ruthie's thought can be, Amorella. This surprising connection with you, a friendly spirit, and my Aunt Ruthie refreshes my soul. I need help explaining why.

Amorella: I cannot explain the phenomena either.

Richard: I should have mentioned Miss Harley and Mr. Stallings, my English freshman and sophomore teachers. There was quite a difference in the way they taught. Miss Harley was very formal and old fashion. I had had elementary teachers like her, and I enjoyed their manner as they dressed the way they presented themselves. Miss Harley was kind, and I could tell which literature she preferred throughout the school year. One of her favorites was Coleridge's *Rime of the Ancient Mariner*. We read the poem out loud, moving down and up the classroom rows. Everyone had her or his turn. Mr. Stallings was an interesting person and he was also advisor for the High Y, a Young Men's Christian organization at school. We got along well. I was chaplain of the High Y for one or two years, I forget which. The girls also had the YWCA equivalent.

After school, Mom took me to the library, and I borrowed the voice record of the poem. I listened to it repeatedly and signed it out for a second week. Miss Harley asked us to memorize lines. I remembered the whole poem and kept it a secret. I am presently listening to a YouTube version with Richard Burton reading the lines. It sounds closest to the record I heard in the Spring of 1956. I did listen to the Burton recording later, without the more recently added music, when it was available, and enjoyed it very much. I listened to the poem several times during my high school years and at least once again privately in sophomore literature in college. Hearing or reading, I always imagined the poem as an accurate tale, not an imaginary one. My heart made the story real and genuine, though my mind knew better.

A Secret Exposed and Accounted for

Amorella: And, here you expose a most personal secret, orndorff. Your heart confirms "The Rime of the Ancient Mariner" is one of your favorite poems in all literature the literature you ever taught. Literature/words are the passion of your heart and, ultimately, your soul. The intellect of Mr. Orndorff has been ruled by his heart. How does that sound, orndorff?

Richard: This is an embarrassment, a shock. No one is to know this because it shows me to be a fraud. For one, I'm glad I am only pretending to be dead and gone. What a waste. I taught college prep, honors, and AP English. That was my profession. I loved the literature I taught. My heart made the words real between the lines, while my mind always knew better, intellectually the poem near the top, but emotionally I have to agree.

Amorella: The immediate question is, why did your intellect allow this most personal deception to take place?

Richard: I hardly ever openly analyzed poems in my classes. I wasn't that helpful on the AP tests. Studying sonnets, some; 17th century, a bit; satire, and heroic couplets, some. Romantic, some, twentieth century, a bit. Chaucer, yes, in some detail – otherwise, not much on the detailed mechanics of poetry. And, from an intellectual viewpoint, I never measured. Strange. I would have thought I would, but I haven't.

I change my mind, Amorella. I wasn't a fraud. I found wit and irony in the best. Some poetry I enjoyed teaching to students more than others. Some of the older students already he irony in their own lives, they didn't have to read it in the poetry or literature. I ran off copies of poems from college literature courses for all my classes. I was not an intellectual, but they understood the irony in the deeper works. Intellectually, I would have been as accepted as an old-fashioned English professor with entirely too much deep digging into literary works. Not in high school or even in the first two years of college English classes. I was not so successful that way. I should have been a more meticulous manager of my time in advanced placement class. That's a regret.

I'll let it go at that. I find this review-of-life-once-lived quite awkward. What's the purpose of such an exercise anyway, when dead. It would be easier if G-D just pronounced (so to speak) a soul going to Hell, a soul to Purgatory, a soul to Heaven, or a soul going to some other place altogether.

Sometimes, I want to tell G-D to piss off and leave me alone. I don't mean G-D; I mean my conscience. Why the hell do I have such a contrary conscience anyway? I sound arrogant and proud, even boastful sometimes, but it is misplaced anger. Time for a break from this shit. Fuck it.

Amorella: *What are you going to do? In here, you are dead, and you don't even have a nose to pick, my man.*

To the Reader, This kind of thing comes up when one is a human spirit and bored even beyond physical death. No one is telling anyone what to do, but people know and understand their own humanity to a point. So, does a spirit do, wait patiently to be reborn? At least life would be something gone through before, even if it is not remembered. – Having a new body and an undeveloped conscious mind, and all kinds of unknown personal and otherwise circumstances to create and/or to live through; it sounds exciting, doesn't it? Or, not?

23 February, 2023, Thursday

Amorella: This morning, you awoke to write this underlined note.

Richard: "If I am dead, I would not need imagination. What would necessitate me to have an imagination? If dead, would there be any need to have curiosity? If dead, what parts of humanity would I need to continue existing spiritually? Why?"

Basically, Amorella, what I am asking is, what parts of being human would not exist without a body and a brain as far as this book is concerned. I am trying to remain realistically plausible to keep my readers' interest.

Amorella: You admit having an ulterior motive for this project. [Distracted, you stay calm by noting the cardinal and his lady waiting to take their turn at the backyard feeder.]

Richard: I want the project to read well for whoever is reading it. You are creating and controlling the conversation to allow me to work on something of my interest, at least that is what it seems to me. For instance, it is assumed that I can ask questions of you as my guardian spirit. Otherwise, what would be the purpose of providing such companionship? How could a spirit-once-human continue to review herorhis life? I would think my questions would not be as far off the norm, statistically speaking, as any other person's questions might be. I cannot imagine, for instance, any human being not having questions once sheorhe realizes herorhis spirit is still in existence after physical death. The project needs continuing within a plausible circumstance – one to which the Readers can relate.

Amorella: I understand your concern. A spirit's humanity will be intact. G-D's gift, the spiritual heart, provides all the functions of spiritual energy for one to remain who she or he was, after physical death. To keep this simple, the soul provides the coating, as it were, for the spiritual heart and memory, etc. No physical features are present. A human spirit's memory understands the five senses. For example, a living person understands the meaning of "a heart's touch" and "a touching, heartfelt scene." Nothing physical but it exists nevertheless. Richard and I conclude this chapter with the definition below.

Note: The High School Experience Continues in the Next Chapter

CONSCIOUSNESS

Opinions differ about what exactly needs to be studied or even considered Consciousness. In some explanations, it is synonymous with the mind and, at other times, an aspect of the mind. In the past, it was one's "inner life," the world of introspection, private thought, imagination, and volition.

Spiritual approaches

To most philosophers, "consciousness" connotes the relationship between the mind and the world. To writers on spiritual or religious topics, it frequently connotes the relationship between the mind and God, or the relationship between the mind and deeper truths that are thought to be more fundamental than the physical world. . ..

Another thorough account of the spiritual approach is Ken Wilber's 1977 book, *The Spectrum of Consciousness,* a comparison of western and eastern ways of thinking about the mind. Wilber described Consciousness as a spectrum with ordinary awareness at one end and more profound understanding at higher levels.

Wikipedia *Selected and Edited by Amorella*

OPEN

Chapter Seven

Continuing with the High School experience.

Richard: The main thing that was important that sophomore year was Latin. We were allowed to read Julius Caesar's *Commentarii de Bello Gallico* [Commentary on the Gallic War]. I borrowed a 'pony' from the Main Branch Columbus Library, which gave the translation from Latin to English. I never considered it cheating because I was sincerely interested in Caesar's work. I knew I needed to understand the Latin language better. I mainly earned Cs. I attempted to read both the Latin and English versions as a single unit out of respect for Caesar as much as for Mrs. Clary. I got caught in class with the translation once and was mortified. I thought Mrs. Clary would banish me from class, and I wouldn't earn the two years of the course I needed if I went on to college. She was kind and allowed me to finish my sophomore year, but I couldn't bring the translation to class. I thanked G-D at the time. I was sure it was divine intervention.

Amorella: You suddenly realize that you believed it to be divine intervention, but you could see no real reason why G-D would do such a thing, so in your big-hearted way, you took the divine intervention as a private friendly gesture and let it go.

Richard: This is such an embarrassing revelation. I should have been struck dead by such a thought. You are right, though. That's close to the way it was. I equated Jesus (and the early idea that I should have a friend in Jesus) with G-D, but I never thought

Jesus was equal to G-D. It didn't make sense; nothing could be equated with G-D but G-D. I realized I was a Jewish thinker, not a Christian. It took me back to the Concentration camps. My soul became Jewish. I kept it to myself. I have not thought about this for the longest time. I made such a connection. But, as usual, I kept it to myself. Besides, it was no one else's business.

Amorella: *Your soul was Jewish?*

Richard: That's what I thought. That's how I resolved the situation at the time. Spiritually, I felt I was as Jewish. Then I let it go. I didn't know about the semantics of metaphysics. I still don't.

Amorella: *Along the way in high school, you had a good speaker during one weekday afternoon, the 1950 winner of the Indianapolis 500, Johnny Parsons. He talked about good save driving, and you took it all in. Then, in your junior year, you bought a well-used gray, stick shift, eight-cylinder 1949 Ford from Wilken Ford on East Main Street in Westerville. The building is still there. Just northwest of the dealership was the water tower. Westerville mostly had Chevy, Ford, Plymouth, and Dodge cars and trucks on its streets and alleys and the car dealers to accompany them.*

Richard: The car took me to the produce department at Albers groceries, where I, a junior, worked with a friend Dwight Bergman in his senior year. I also used the car to visit my friends Doug, Don, and Fritz during those years. Unfortunately, I had an accident with the vehicle. Tom Fletcher was with me, and we were heading back to Minerva Park after football practice.

Marjory, one of my classmates, was riding her horse south off State Street after the railroad track. The horse shied out as I was about to pass, and its rear end slid up my right front fender and cracked my windshield. Marjory was thrown off and taken to the hospital. She and her horse survived.

After the police, ambulance, and taking care of the horse were completed, I drove home, first dropping off Tom. Marjory was back in school mending a broken arm a few days later. Marjory sat across from me in homeroom during my junior year.

I was quite discombobulated by the whole incident. Marjory was friendly and polite. I felt terrible, even guilty, for the awkward situation. That's what Aunt Ruthie and Aunt Patsy would have said. I tried to get by saying little about the incident, but my friends, had a field day with jokes and so forth, which made me triple embarrassed (if such an expression is allowed these days).

Richard: At the termination of my senior year, I wanted to thank all my teachers personally. All are listed in the yearbooks. I may not remember the teachers' names, but I remember the politeness, the kindness, and the personal caring they showed. I love my teachers. I love my friends.

Amorella: This is one example of how it is when conscious life is over. Remembrance. That's why Richard's recently seemingly dead heartansoulanmind flows through his life with me as his spirit guide.

Richard: Something else comes to heart – the senior year was the best of the years in Westerville City Schools. We were all friends; if not, it seemed we were all friends. At eighteen, my senior year is my life's happiest, most joyous year. At eighty-one years old, these memories are deep in my heart. 'I love you, the Westerville Class of 1960. We had sad times and good times like all other class years. We were the last to graduate from Westerville High School on South State Street.'

Amorella: You were in the school auditorium. The girls wore white robes over their dressy clothes and a flower; the boys wore red robes over their better clothes. You could see everyone's cleaned up or new shoes. Parents, grandparents, other families, and friends clapped as each walked across the stage. With this, we conclude Chapter Five and move on to the next chapter.

Richard: Being as dead, I feel like I am living in a personal "Our Town" segment by Thornton Wilder.

Amorella: First, we define the heart, then the soul.

DEFINITIONS:

Heart - noun 1• The heart is regarded as the center of a person's thoughts and emotions, especially love, compassion, or loyalty: hardening his heart, he ignored her entreaties | he poured out his heart to me | she had already given her heart to another | he has no heart. • one's mood or feeling: they had a change of heart. • courage or enthusiasm: they may lose heart as the work mounts up | Mary took heart from the encouragement handed out | I put my heart and soul into it and got fired.

New Oxford English American Dictionary

Amorella: Below is the definition of the "soul" from Wikipedia, with which you feel more comfortable.

Soul – noun - **1** the spiritual or immaterial part of a human being or animal, regarded as immortal: they believe death is just one step in a soul's journey through the universe. • a person's moral or emotional nature or sense of identity: in the depths of her soul, she knew he would betray her.

New Oxford English American Dictionary

Richard: I realize it was stupid to designate my soul as Jewish when the soul is an essence.

Amorella: You gave up the argument when you could have just as easily sarcastically said the Jewish word 'neshamah' for breath rather than use 'essence'.

Richard: You are right once again, Amorella, more so because I was only going to write the Jewish word 'neshamah' without adding 'sarcastically.'

Amorella: The two above statements show how words can be used to define something that exists in hypothesis and theory only. You had this problem come up earlier in your life, and when you finally decided to do something about it, you dropped the 'o' out of the English spelling or G-D. You followed others' concepts but did treat both ends with capital for balance and clarification.

Richard: This leads me to believe that if we cannot write a word for G-D, then how do we write any word that defines something metaphysical and do the meaning justice? Heart, Soul, and Mind used in context, separately and together, are non-existing in physical formats. We accept this without much effort. We accept ghost as a word and spirit as noun.

We make suggestions things are accurate when the items do not exist. By nature, human beings are deceptive, even in capturing observations of who or what we are. This is when we are alive. How are these deceptions eliminated if we communicate in whatever way when we are spirits alone? Does consciousness alone take the place of words? How is the word 'thought' accepted as a whole piece? What do we do if our realities cannot be made clear to one another?

We do what we do now, muddle through. But, when we are individual spirits alone, what do we muddle through, consciousness? Strangely, I reasoned G-D's existence while alive in my consciousness. How is this possible?

Amorella: Human consciousness allows that you are alive, and you may accept you are with your heartansoulanmind. Similarly, when no longer active. Suppose one still recognizes this without any physical properties. In that case, one is spiritually alive because sheorhe acquired consciousness by/with becoming born [life] and is allowed to keep herorhis consciousness when dead.

Richard: I do not accept G-D as consciousness, even with a capital on Consciousness. G-D is G-D. Is this the kind of thing the Dead debate?-

Amorella: Evidently so, orndorff.

Richard: Then I must complete my task first. Study and accept my life – and come up with a new personal name of approximately 150 words that show others who I am now that I am dead.

Amorella: In this book, G-D has a sense of humor.

Richard: I accept this sense of humor wholeheartedly.

Amorella: Good. So, do I. But, as a species, living or dead, human beings are not the source of a joke. If you were, you would not laugh so good-humoredly.

Richard: Now, that is a fascinating comment, Amorella. You showed me something here, I just realized now. We are not the source of the joke. What a notion to imply.

Amorella: I said, 'human beings are not the source of the joke,' as an impromptu aside, orndorff. Nothing was meant by it.

Richard: I re-read the above from yesterday. I misunderstood, "We are not the joke's source. "In the line beginning with the earlier line, you say," Good. So, do I. But, as a species, living or dead, we are not the source of a joke. If we were, we would not laugh at it good-humoredly. In the earlier line, you say, "G-D has a sense of humor."

Amorella: Yes, of course. This fictional philosophically inspired work is not a philosophical course on the 'Nature of G-D,' orndorff.

Richard: Should I delete the timed line and beyond, including this line? It has thrown off my thinking. It would be better to delete it.

Amorella: No, it is an example of your honest nature as a 'journalistic spirit.'

Richard: The journal aspect shows I have confusions, which is the whole reason for the book l in the first place, to iron out the mess. When confused, I find it better to write the details out so I can read them before me and not try to read them in my mind, where I muddle things up. Maybe my heart muddles concepts of this nature, not my mind. Either way, I have built-in confusion issues to mend.

Amorella: Following your lead here, it makes a difference regarding the source of the confusion.

Richard: How is this so? The heart and mind are equal and are allowed immortality, at least from my perspective in here.

Amorella: In response to your question, the spiritual heart is a gift from G-D; the mind is, first, a gift from Nature.

Richard: Interesting; I had not considered this. I now understand and accept this statement as is. The mind develops from the physical brain and body, and the heart comes with the soul.

Amorella: You found the Hindi, Christian, and Jewish definitions of 'heart.' I use Jewish as it fits the nature of this work.

Richard: Amorella, I am still determining what is essential in the spiritual and the physical human being and what is not critical in this work.

Amorella: I am your guide, orndorff. I am here to help you find yourself so you can be renamed among many other heartsansoulsanminds. This work is not a theological study. No one can correctly pronounce you Jewish, Christian, or any other religious organization. You are dead. Do you think the Dead concern themselves holy? This is a private matter. Everyone who is physically dead has a spiritual heartansoulanmind that contemplates. Once one finishes this task and comes up with a new name for her or himself – a name to use among old and new friends, it will be enough for this exercise.

OPEN

Chapter Eight

The Trip West

Amorella: In mid-June, 1960, three graduating seniors of the Westerville Class of 1960, Gary Jackson, George Miles and George Musson and yourself, borrowed your father's 1952 green Willys Jeep Station Wagon and took a month or so trip from Westerville to St. Louis, Oklahoma City, the Grand Canyon, Los Vegas, Los Angeles, San Diego, Tijuana, up to Los Angeles, Santa Cruz, San Francisco, Sacramento, Reno, the Salt Lake City, The Grand Teton National Park, Yellowstone National Park, the Badlands, Kansas City, Independence, Missouri, St. Louis, Indianapolis, Columbus and Westerville. There were four major incidents you had not experienced before.

One. Along Will Roger's freeway before Oklahoma City, the jeep would not move forward, so you turned it around off-the-highway itself, and backed it into Oklahoma City near the side of the road, where the carbonator was readjusted at a Willys acceptable garage for higher altitudes.

Two. You four walked to the bottom of the Grand Canyon with a canteen of water each. You almost died from dehydration. The service rangers found out from others who passed you on the trail to Phantom Ranch. It took you a second day and half the night to walk out after fellow travelers shared their sandwiches and water.

Three. You got lost trying to find Disney World and had to sleep on the side of a road near the freeway. You awoke discovering a bear had 'ramshackled' everything looking for food, then pooped and peed on your sleeping bag. The others thought it was quite *funny. You bathed by a sink at a nearby gas station restroom and changed clothes.*

Four. *After Disney World you drove to Tijuana. None of you spoke Spanish well. You only had Latin to go by. You bought gifts, pots, to take back to family. On the way out of Tijuana you had a flat tire and had to take most everything out of the car to get the spare. While putting on the spare the jack slipped and smash the presents you had bought.*

Five. *Once you eventually reached your Aunt Fran and Uncle Dee Schick's house near Santa Cruz your Aunt Fran would not let any of you in the house until after each hosed off in the back yard. Uncle Dee was kinder but wondered how you four survived, being as inexperienced as you were. Aunt Fran was much better when you had cleaned up and had two spare rooms for sleeping. While staying with the Schick's you traveled to the coast for a swim in the Pacific.*

When you arrived at a beach in mid-morning you found it mostly deserted and with some rough waves, but it didn't denture you. You decided to go further out and the others were waving to you, so you waved back. Almost immediately as you turned around you felt a great pressure on chest, hips and legs. The next thing you knew was you were standing, and the water was gone except below your ankles. You looked up and this wave, at least twelve feet high loomed not more than three feet away. You took a deep breath and suddenly you felt like you were in a washing machine spin cycle. Any time you saw blue sky you took an immediate took a breath and let nature does its work. Eventually, you found yourself down the beach, and you begin to crawl and then stand somewhat. You made your way to shore as the others ran down the beach towards you.

Later, your Aunt Fran said you could have been drowned in the undertow. You had understood the word 'undertow' but did not understand the implications while in the water. The undertow experience changed your sense of what living is. Nature can be uncontrollable and is deserves your respect. That is what you learned. The rest of the trip was an enjoyable adventure, more of what you expected the whole trip to be.

Amorella: *Late summer, 1960, you moved from your grandparents on the corner of Knox and Walnut to Middleburg Heights, a southwest suburb of Cleveland. Your father had already built you a bedroom on the west side of the basement with flooring. You got a laborer's job at Foseco, Inc., where your father was a metallurgist and manager. You worked full-time from September into May 1961.*

Richard: During Fall and Winter, I took two literature night classes at Fenn College on Cleveland's East Side. Fenn College later became a part of Cleveland State University. I earned Cs in both classes. I wasn't cut out for college. Spring of 1962, I decided to leave home abruptly one morning in May. I left a one-page note on the kitchen table head and hitchhiked west thinking of becoming a lone mountain man type of character and surviving by doing odd jobs, somewhat on the order of Henry David Thoreau of Concord, Mass. He was a hero.

Amorella: *You cannot recall much about the fiasco in bumming your way to Denver from Cleveland other than you got a ride to Columbus and from Columbus, you had several rides across Indiana, Illinois, Missouri, Kansas, and into Denver. All were uneventful, but one where the fellow in the stretches of Kansas was somewhat drunk and speeding, and you told him you*

87

wanted out. He ignored you until you pulled an eight-inch brown leather blackjack from your jacket pocket. Grandma Schick had given you the weapon when Popo Schick died because you thought it was neat weapon. He had it when he hunted revenuers in southern Ohio. You had that blackjack when you began teaching and kept it hidden but carried it if you thought there might be an altercation while walking along a city street alone.

Richard: I spent about a month at a sleazy hotel near downtown Denver while trying to join the United States Air Force. I took and passed the tests for officer training but never passed the physical because of high blood pressure and other issues, I think flat feet. I was running out of money, so with no other foreseeable recourse, I took a Greyhound bus from Denver back to Columbus. Grandma and Grandpa Orndorff allowed me to stay with them. After that, my parents said I had to find a job to stay.

I was allowed to stay at Knox and Walnut and got a summer job at Blendon Township, where a relative, Harold Freeman, was one of the Township elected officials. That Fall, I entered Otterbein College on probation. I assume I was accepted because my father and other relatives had graduated from Otterbein, I worked for a year to save the money for college, and I did not need room and board. I quickly found part-time employment at the local bookstore, and Grandma Orndorff got me a Saturday night job bussing tables at the popular Grandview Inn in Columbus, where she was the head chef.

Amorella: You became a first-year student but were genuinely connected with Otterbein when you pledged to the old 1908, Pi Kappa Phi or Country Club at 79 South Grove Street. This is a city block from your grandparent's home at 103 West Walnut Street. Some of your active Brothers were your Class of 1960. Your father had been an active Clubber in his day, which also helped. You ended up with a C in Western Civilization and Chemistry and a D in Spanish. The two bright spots were Bs in English and Physical Education.

Richard: Walking to school from Grandma's house: head west on Walnut, pass the cemetery, right on Grove, pass the fraternity, pass the President's house on the southwest side of Grove and Park, straight on Park to Grove and College, turn left, walk west thirty yards or so and enter the doors of Towers Hall, that's where English 101 with Mr. Thackery was located. I could have World History first, then Western Civilization. Western Civilization was in a brick Arts building directly across from the Administration Building on the southeast corner of College Avenue. It's now a parking lot. Spanish was in Towers Hall, second floor, and the lab with headphones was there. The brick Physical Education was in the brick building west of Towers along Park Street. Chemistry was on the first floor of the brick Science building west of Towers along College Street.

Amorella: Two recent historical events in the 1960s also deeply affected your spiritual life in those earlier college days. One was the Cuban Missile Crisis, and the other the President Kennedy's assassination.

Richard: I don't think either one had that much effect on me personally, not enough to reflect on while being recently dead. The Cuban Missile Crisis had a doomsday setting, but I was already depressed, like the world going to hell in a handbasket. If we survived that crisis, there would always be another to flare. Eventually, we were all going to die anyway. The Kennedy assassination affected me because it was blatantly unfair that such a good young man was killed in such a shocking way. The killing was for no good reason. The same can be said for Bob Kennedy's assassination.

Amorella. *So, if the assassinations had been for a good reason, was it okay to do so?*

Richard: People tried to assassinate Hitler. It might have shortened the war on the European front if they had.

Amorella: *Even now, some recently dead cannot let World War II go.*

Richard: I hadn't thought about it, Amorella. I don't know how people personally affected by war will just let it go after death. How can the dead let that go within any personal settings of revenge or just outright hate? Where is the fairness and justice in that? I think I have gotten off track here, Amorella.

In time I can let things go, perhaps even consciously forget about them long before I can forgive them. I'm not thinking about everyday things between people, but events like murder or deliberately killing someone and having no remorse. I can't believe this topic ever came up. Forgiving someone for something heinous will help the forgiver, I'm sure.

Letting such emotions as hate, revenge, and jealousy go is the only way to regain one's freedom and dignity to lead a better life. There is no other choice. Perhaps, that is where the personal anger lies rooted, in the fact that there is no other choice but to let hate, revenge, and jealousies go and stop blaming G-D go also. People seem to always want to blame someone else for their troubles. People need to grow up. People grow up and then grow old. One way or another, they eventually die. . I'd like to be out of here with freedom, dignity, and grace. That's how I'd like to die.

Amorella: The recently dead can do this too, move on with freedom, dignity, and grace. Each must find herorhis own way.

Richard: This means freedom, dignity, and grace are goals gained while discovering oneself through reflecting on what life was. Time and the revolving motions and emotions were literally a one-time snap. Once time and space are out of the equation, the only things left are the reason, thought, and considerations. The dead are an intellectual lot once they have resolved their lives and decided on a new name for who they are presently, recently departed.

Amorella: What did you do in your personal off time in those college days? You became a Beatnik, one of possibly two on campus. You wore shades, longer hair, a trimmed beard, wrote poetry, and read dark European philosophies while wearing sweatshirts inside out most everywhere, shorts when the weather permitted, and sandals or shoes with no socks and a black beret from France. You were in the dark shadows of your mind so much that you felt at home there. Of course, you might have committed suicide, but what would you do? Heart-wise, you felt like a worthless piece of shit. Does that sound about right, orndorff?

Richard: That's brutal, Amorella. I'm sure I didn't appear that way publicly. Otterbein would have kicked me out, as well as our fraternity standards would. But I did feel that way. I had no far-reaching goals other than traveling around Europe, which I never did. I was a Beatnik in my mind, no question about it. I loved European philosophers of the seventeenth through the twentieth century. I still love words and their varied meanings in and out of context. Letters, words and grammar in general are an entanglement within my heartansoulanmind.

Amorella: Socially, you did have a wonderful and enthusiastically positive girlfriend along the way

Richard: Jean was my friend and a fellow English major, and my age, but a year ahead in school. She was always busy in a good way. I admire her still. Jean had goals and worked for them. She wanted to be a teacher of English. She helped and guided me to be a better student. We went to a few fraternity/ sorority dances and such. Jean was an officer in Epsilon Kappa Tau sorority. We were friends and had good times together. Later, after she graduated and was teaching in a high school in California, I asked her to marry me at Christmas time.

Jean conditionally accepted the ring but told me she had a boyfriend in California. I was immature but didn't realize how much so. My second cousin David helped talk me out of the possible marriage. I asked for the ring back in early February. Jean sent the ring back. I was not doing well in school and realized I would not graduate with my class in 1965. I needed to grow up, have a more significant life purpose, and graduate. I finally did graduate in 1967. Jean had married her California boyfriend. I remember Jean all these years. She died a couple of years ago. I am glad we were such good friends in those college years, and I hope we still are. I know she felt this way because she told an old mutual friend to pass the note on to me before she died. Life is interesting. This is not a cliché, especially here.

Amorella: How so?

Richard: I found the reference to her imagining we would meet again as the friends we always were in college buried in my older computer recently. I had forgotten where the reference was. I am writing about death, and the memory comes up most unexpectedly. I'm glad it did. This leaves me wondering. What is *real* here? Is this reconnection ironic, or what? This is one of those real moments, Amorella.

Is the wonderment of the moment confusing? Or am I confused? Here such a moment, right here, right now. My mind and intellect say, "Surely not, grow up, orndorff. You never want to grow up." But, my heart of hearts says, "Jean and I are friends. We love one another. We will always love one another." Why is this considered so wrong? I cannot deny my heart. I will always love my wife, Carol, also. That is not considered wrong. Damn culture. I love both in different ways. I love other friends along with Carol, also in different ways. I consider Carol a friend first, because she is. Carol is a marriage pardner second. Friends are first. It would be unethical to be lovers and not friends first. How could one be a lover first and a friend second? That does not make sense to me.

I have already written about how much I love my friend, my companion for all these years, my wife, Carol. Love is not the right word here, Amorella. This needs to be clarified. Alas, this is a secret intimate, almost 'un-sharable' part of my heart. Some aspects of consciousness are not sharable because they are in a wordless reality between heart and mind. I feel emotion with both the heart and mind, I try to 'feel' equally, but if, as you say, Amorella, 'the heart is a gift from G-D, and the mind is a gift from Nature,' we human beings are formed with both heart and mind. Heart and mind are not equal. By definition here, to me, the heart is stronger because of the Giver, G-D.

I enjoy creating this experiment with you Amorella. My question is still unresolved. This Journal is a reality because it can be seen or read. But between the lines in these two paragraphs, what is the reality? [Pause] My answer is, humility. This chapter is a necessary lesson for me, I don't know whether it is necessary for the Readers. They must imagine and resolve their own stories of being.

Amorella: No one else is here, orndorff, just you and me. You don't need the drama.

Richard: Humility is not drama Amorella. Arrogance is. I am shutting up to relax.

Amorella: That's one of the beauties of this Place of the Dead, orndorff. It's timeless. And, this is a good place to end the chapter.

OPEN

Chapter Nine

26 February 2023, Sunday

Richard: It's February 1965. I work on graduation part-time because I am mostly out of money. The independent courses I'm taking are one and two-hour semester classes that I create, and Dr. John Coulter okays and accepts I will do. I am responsible for the readings and a ten to fifteen-page paper. One course is titled Eugene O'Neil, and the plays were: *Emperor Jones* and *The Hairy Ape*. The other course was Milton's *Paradise Lost*. I had one discussion period with Dr. Coulter on each subject, but I needed to remember the exact thesis of each. I compared the two plays to modern tragedies. Milton's lofty goals were far above O'Neil's, but they should not have been reached and should have been in the papers. Milton's settings in *Paradise Lost, Paradise Regained*, and *Samson Agonistes* were otherworldly, just as Dante's *Inferno, Purgatorio,* and *Paradiso* were. Even earlier, Virgil wrote *Aeneid* about the adventures of Aeneas. All three worked within the theme of otherworldly circumstances. I have long been interested in stories about human beings communicating with celestial beings. Fate and Free come into play as themes of Good and Evil also. Justice and Fairness also. Fear and Favor are two others. Reason and Belief are two more. I feel I need more conceptualizations here.

On a critical level, This is my almost irrational fear of not making myself understood. When writing mythology about gods and human beings, there is an imaginary dread I would misunderstand a god or goddess if I ran into one on Mount Olympus, for example. As for communicating with an angel or angel-like creature or a possible imaginary being, well, in sharing with you, Amorella, the only thing I can do is let all this fear and inner conflict go and rely on you to understand what I am attempting to communicate at one given time or another. Telepathic communication of a sort. This works for me, Amorella.

Amorella: This is because we communicate through heart and reason simultaneously. . . in words and between the lines, so to speak. You see, orndorff, this communication between us is a bit of heaven to you, whether it is fiction or not.

Richard: I am not being scholarly. I will be seen as a fool if I am not academic or intellectual in intent.

Amorella: You have hit a simple truth about yourself. This is a greater self-conflict than you think. The above thought guided you through teaching students every day of your life. This is the fear, "I will make a fool of myself. I will be humiliated and fired. If I can't teach, my only other satisfactory employment would be digging graves.

Richard: "My only self-worth is in teaching young people or digging graves."

Amorella: So, there you have it, orndorff, almost forty years of your professional life resting on these words.

Amorella: No twilight zone is pushed or pulled by a steam engine without some imagination, old man.

Richard: The only thing I get out of that comment is quantum physics and physics show a displacement lacking some imagination, Amorella. Otherwise, I have yet to learn what you are talking about.

Amorella: My thought took less than a minute. Yours took four.

Richard: Why is it you can think faster than I do?

Amorella: I, the Amorella, have no physics.

Richard: The dead have no physics either. I don't think of spirituality as being without physics. It is not observed consciously, at least. I believe the opposite of a spiritual world is a material world.' The construction of that sentence could be more comfortable. The opposite of a spiritual world is a secular world.

Amorella: Yet both exist in the same space.

Richard: One is time. The other appears timeless.

Amorella: Timelessness is imagination, not reality, to the living.

Richard:

1. Timelessness is a construction, not imagination, Amorella.

2. What is the reason for this exercise, other than human beings don't come entirely constructed, or perhaps the heartansoulanmind is not fully constructed?

3. What does the heartansoulanmind displace in the dimension of space?

4. Is the heartansoulanmind alone/by itself complete, or not complete?

5. You have stirred up these questions in my mind, Amorella. I am still trying to understand why? – I am tired, enough for tonight.

Amorella: *I agree. Tomorrow then.*

27 February 2023, Monday

Richard: I must feed the cats and get ready to meet Kim at the doctor's office. I want to say my new doctor's name is Babbage, but it isn't. The name starts with a B and reflects Henry II of England, though, when the man whose name I can't remember was Archbishop and assassinated by people who thought they were doing the king's bidding. – Beckett, Thomas Beckett. Beckett must be the new-to-me doctor's name. I'll find out soon enough.

Amorella: *You arrived home, ate breakfast, and read the paper. Dr. Will Beckett, M.D. pronounced your health pretty good overall, considering you are eighty and weigh 263 pounds. He suggested seeing a physical therapist, and you replied you disliked seeing one. Kim said she would go with you, so you* *reluctantly agreed to go sometime soon. You will see Kim for breakfast tomorrow morning, something you are willing to do. Raining straight down has begun in earnest. The house is mostly ready for the cleaning people.*

Richard: I remembered who Babbage was at the Lewis Center road roundabout on the way to the doctor's office. He was an English actor at the time of Shakespeare or during the 18th century. I have not found out why I associated him with Becket except for the first letter.

Checking Wikipedia, I found Richard Burbage was the most famous stage actor at the Globe Theatre. Charles Babbage, however, was "a mathematician, philosopher, inventor, and mechanical engineer who also originated the concept of the digital programmable computer." He lived from December 1791 into October 1871. This leads me to wonder how spiritual memory would help me out after death.

Amorella: Must you be reminded this book is not projecting a reality of how human consciousness is after death. This is staged so the Reader, yourself first, might better comprehend how consciousness might reasonably be within the assumingly immortal heartansoulanmind after physical death.

Richard: Writing unconsciously allows me to forget the actual reality of living. I know better when consciously awakened, as you did for me in the abovementioned paragraph. I become/ am in a 'reality-of-the-linear-moment' setting when writing. I need a break. Damn, I just ate the rest of that eight-ounce can of cashews setting beside me. I can't believe ten minutes just went by.

Amorella: What you think while writing is sometimes what you are presently, orndorff.

Richard: I just awakened from a nap. I was sitting in the brown chair in the bedroom and rubbing my face. In my heartansoulanmind stands Albert Fields. First, the Sound of Music comes first memory; second, Bert lived across the street from 103 West Walnut in the first house north on the corner of Knox Street. Bert was a Clubber like myself but from sophisticated Chicago. He was my first friend from somewhere other than the Westerville area.

Bert and I developed a special relationship based on honesty, trust, and friendship. We sometimes would go up Knox Street to the College Inn, a small restaurant near the corner of Knox and College, across from the First Presbyterian Church. The relaxed restaurant style suited Bert, who found himself Uptown, usually drinking coffee at the Inn. He became friends with the kind, older lady, the owner. I don't remember drinking coffee, but he showed me it was an excellent place to relax and refresh in the busyness of being single in college. I was in a Beatnik phase. And Bert and the College Inn suited me well.

Bert liked to play golf with fellow Clubbers Jim Shumaker, Craig Brelsford, David Short, and Bob Clawson. Jim was from Colorado Springs, but he had lived in Westerville until he was six when his family moved out west. I quickly slipped into a friendship with Jim too. His parents and my parents knew each other well because in the 1930s Westerville was still a small town where everyone knew everyone else, whether they wanted to or not.

In 1965, *The Sound of Music* came out, and we took an afternoon to see it. We were enthralled with the story, the characters, the setting, the dialogue, and the music. We were more than enthralled; we were 'charmed' by the whole production. I am thinking of the Middle English definition of 'charmed' here, as in the human sense of an incantation of a magic spell. Over the next month or so, we saw the film at least eight times, maybe more. One time we serendipitously took a day trip up to Windsor, Ontario, just to get out of Westerville and talked about the film most of the way. Then after lunch at a diner in Windsor, we drove back. It was a wonderfully free, very human day, completely spontaneous. Bert and I went everywhere in my new VW. Popo Orndorff bought the car for me that Spring. He loaned me the money, and I paid him back once I began teaching.

One day Bert asked me to take him to the VW dealer, where he bought a beautiful car, a green Karman Kia convertible with a brown top. We went into the Midwest Volkswagen car dealer, and Bert looked over the vehicles, pointed, and said, "I want that one." The dealer smiled. We obviously looked like students. Bert said he wanted that car that afternoon. He had the check the check to buy it. Things settled down quickly. Bert stayed and waited. I drove back home. Later, in the afternoon, he came over, and we took a ride in his new car. That is the only time I have ever witnessed someone buying a car outright other than when my favorite grandpa, Popo, purchased my car at the same dealer. I paid him back.

During winter break in 1966, Popo Orndorff wanted to see an old friend who had retired and was living along the Florida east coast. So, we took my 1965 green VW to Florida. I invited Bert, and he drove with us in his Karman Ghia. We kept track of one another with walkie-talkies we already had and used them as telephones between our houses.

We had a wonderful time. We traveled down I-75, where it was completed, and took the old route south when we had no choice. We drove down through Atlanta and into Florida. We took the west coast to Tampa, from Tampa to Naples, then across the Everglades Parkway, crossing through Seminole Tribe lands. Finally, we stopped at a small village. With all the warm weather and quickly forgetting what season we were in, Popo asked what the people did in the winter. We three had a good laugh.

From Miami, we drove up the east coast where I-95, like I-75, still needed completed. We stopped and visited his friend in Pompano Beach. We listened as the two old-timers recollected. Once again traveling, we stopped at Cape Canaveral and the future John F. Kennedy space center. We drove right up to the enormous building which would hold the rocket, parked, got out, walked into the empty building, and looked around. No one stopped us. Very cool, it was.

From there, we went up to St. Augustine, stopping to see the sights. Popo was enthralled the whole trip. Bert and I enjoyed it too. Then, we headed west to I-75 and home to Westerville and Otterbein before classes began. Bert graduated from Otterbein with a major in economics and married Mary. Our close friendship waned but has not been forgotten. Our friendship was a natural part of maturing and moving on, which was what life was all about, or so it seemed.

Amorella: This is a good place to stop.

OPEN

Chapter Ten

8 March 2023, Wednesday

Amorella: 'Stub Born' Freak *went down along an underlined-up path is the first sentence of your new name for now.*

Richard: I made it up with humor; and, amazingly, with Grace alone.

Amorella: I will stop your new name for today. Your new name is: "Stub Born Freak went down along an underlined-up path. I made the name up with humor and, amazingly, with Grace alone."

Richard: I cannot tell if you are joking, Amorella.

Amorella: Good. Now, you can go back to sleep.

Richard: Do you want to call me Stub Born Freak instead of Richard?

Amorella: Where is your mind, boy? This is fiction. Can't you tell the difference?

Richard: I can, but this is in the book, so I needed clarification. That's the reason I asked. I, like Hamlet, "know a hawk from a handsaw."

Amorella: Do you know where this material is coming from in your mind?

Richard: I think so; I mean, it is a line from Shakespeare's *Hamlet*; I just looked it up because I forgot the word 'hawk.'

Amorella: I mean in your head, orndorff.

Richard: Okay. You mean, why did I come up with the quotation in the first place. – My leaning at present is that with a beginning name like that, this is not a tragedy, Amorella.

People aren't going to change their names to some one hundred and fifty words after they die; they aren't crazy. I'm not, either. Like everyone else, I will wait until I am physically dead to see what happens. I'm not even positive the heartansoulanmind exists like it does in our book. I can't afford to think of this as a plausible reality. I don't have the faith to believe in that way.

Amorella: Stub Born is honest. 'Freak went' is a joke. I give that to you, boy. In here, you stay Richard, and your headstone says Richard, no need to waste your money getting the headstone changed.

Richard: someone other than me is the right person to write this. I only had one or two courses in philosophy. I'm not Karl Marx or Martin Luther. I was a grave digger and a teacher. I'm willing to let it go at that. I could add that to our gravestone, but some would consider it disrespectful to Carol. I think she would find it mildly funny but also a stupid thing to do, so I won't.

Besides, you're not even an Angel or a pretend angel in this work. You are a kind spirit, and I am gratefully appreciative of this. You said you are a composite of two compatible spiritual human hearts. I can accept that without faith or belief, but as humans are prone to error, consistently human hearts may also be in error from time to time.

Amorella: Do you want me to become, as it were, an Angel, like Gabriel, for instance?

Richard: Hell no, Amorella. That would scare the shit out of me if I believed it, and if you convinced anyone else, it could be like Hell on Earth, or worse, because of the crazies in the world who might think the end is near.

Amorella: Another frank bit of honesty. You are a good fellow, orndorff. I have no doubts; I accept you at your word. Time for a break. Later, dude.

Richard: I wish you would quit doing this, Amorella. I get confused enough. But fortunately for me, these are but haphazard thoughts.

Amorella: You hit that on the button, my man.

Richard: I don't understand what 'on the button' means.

Amorella: Good, perhaps our Readers will.

Amorella: You are looking north towards the pine trees at Westerville Park. Quite a few people are out. Two couples are sitting on the blanket having lunch and enjoying the sun through the light haze; that is how it appears. You can never take anything for granted, can you, orndorff?

Richard: I take you for what you say you are, Amorella. I will never take any of this next adventure for granted. I met Carol. It was the Fall of 1965, and my sister, Cathy, and Carol had moved into Kings Hall at Otterbein. I was not there when they moved in.

Cathy said our mother and father were in the room when Carol showed up with her parents, Scotch and Jean. Our parents had wondered if Carol was Jean and Scotch's daughter; of course, it quickly became apparent.

Cathy noted the first time I met Carol was when Cathy called me and wanted a ride down to Ohio State to see some of her Cleveland friends. Carol decided to go along, so I met her when I picked up Cathy. That's Cathy's recollection. It sounds reasonable.

All I remember was that whenever it was, Carol sat in my VW's backseat behind Cathy because I could see Carol in the rearview mirror. I'm embarrassed that I don't remember beyond that. Carol appeared charming and young, and I remember thinking, 'There was no way Carol would be attracted to the likes of me anyway.' I dismissed any idea of a relationship between us out of hand.

Amorella: That next to the last and last sentence are exactly you.

Richard: We were formally introduced at the beginning of that car ride to the Ohio State University. Later, within the month, I heard about Cathy and Carol walking from Kings Hall to Towers Hall. They walked under a tree near the Science Hall, and a squirrel dumped a load on Carol.

In the afternoon, Carol told me about the incident. I started to laugh. Carol transfigured into a waspish rage; the ever-polite facade simply vanished. I observed Carol's unwashed and honest self, and she didn't mix words. Carol Jean Hammond unknowingly drilled deep into my heart's depths at that moment. I quickly sensed my laugh caused her abrupt embarrassment and anger. The reason for my laughter was that I had figuratively felt shit on plenty of times, and her unfortunate mishap, mysteriously and instantly had now become one of my own.

Amorella: The empathy puts you within her private person. She was a pent-up angry person, as were you and still are. You both privately share a deeply secret anger about life's unforeseen circumstances, but you were and are not angry with each other, per se. As a good friend told you the other day, "You and Carol still enjoy holding hands; that's true love."

Richard: Isn't that something. I never thought that in my entire conscious life. Shared anger; what a basis for a lifetime of mutual friendship. I agree; it is true love in any case. How is that possible?

Amorella: You have nothing more to say?

Richard: I am speechless.

Amorella: Let's stop here.

Amorella: What is the next important event you remember?

Richard: Later that Fall, 1965, Carol and I drove to Jimmy Shumaker's grandfather's apartment a block north of old Emerson Junior High and watched the end of the Cleveland Browns playing the New York Giants. Carol and I stopped to say hello. That's when Carol met some of my friends, Craig Brelsford, Jim Shumaker, and Bob Clawson. The four of us were enthusiastic Browns fans in those days.

Amorella: This is how friendships work within the heartsansoulsanminds of the dead. A heartansoulanmind asks telepathic-like to one of her once living friends who was a witness to a shared event. This heartansoulanmind reflects on the memory of the circumstance like you did yesterday when you called Cathy and asked a question about when the squirrel incident took place. Then you called Craig to find out who was at Jim's grandfather's when you introduced Carol. Friends share memories. Why? Each reinforces the other to remember the circumstance or event more clearly. Conversations relating to personal memory lighten things up.

Richard: Why change your names when you are physically dead?

Amorella: You don't forget your old name to meet new friends with unshared experiences more quickly. Old friends call you by your old name like always.

Amorella: Cathy left Otterbein at the end of the first semester. She returned to Cleveland to continue her undergraduate work at Cleveland State, where Tod, her boyfriend of seven years, was already studying. Carol acquired another roommate to finish out the school year. This allowed you plenty of time to cultivate a stronger, more serious relationship. That summer between her First and Second Year, Carol was home in Alexandria, Virginia, a suburb near Washington, D.C. Her father, Dr. Grandville "Scotch" Hammond, a former public-school superintendent in Alliance, Ohio, held a high non-political State Department USAID post helping South Vietnam develop a more efficient and better public educational system from primary through the university level.

Richard: This same summer, my friend, Bob Pringle, married Patti Hague in May 1966 at the United Methodist Church on State Street in Westerville. This is while Bob was in dental school at Ohio State. I was the best man, an honor I've never forgotten. Bob and Patti lived on Thirteenth Avenue, off High Street, near the university. We made it a point to see each other from time to time. Times were changing, Bob was married, and I had a girlfriend.

Amorella: Carol invited you to visit as she worked at Woodward & Lothrop or Woodie's, a department store in downtown Washington in the summer. In early June, you took off your summer work with the City of Westerville to visit.

113

Richard: I was excited and terrified, both at once. I last went to Washington when I was five or six. This would be the most extended road trip I had ever taken. I was methodical in following the map, planning fuel stops, etc. In those days, it would be about a seven-and-a-half-hour trip from Westerville to Alexandria, Virginia, because the freeways were not entirely constructed, and the very busy Pennsylvania Turnpike was only two lanes each way, of course there were fewer cars, but plenty of trucks.

I arrived about four-thirty in the afternoon. When I knocked on the door, Carol's father answered. I assumed it would be her mother. Dr. Hammond gave a friendly hello and opened the door wide so I might enter. He told me Carol would be home from work soon and asked if I wanted to freshen up. Only then did I realize I appeared hot and sweaty. I had not fully used the car air conditioning to save gas, and I had the windows down in front, and the back windows popped out. It was a hotter, more humid day in the Washington D.C. area than it had been coming across the Allegany mountains of Pennsylvania.

I didn't understand what Carol's father meant by "freshen up." Was I supposed to shower and change clothes before Carol arrived? I had no idea, but shortly after that, Carol arrived in the driveway, with her mother driving in their blue and white 1965 Ford Crown Victoria. 'Halleluiah,' shouted my heartanmind.

When the two walked through front doorway, there were a lot of smiles accompanied by friendly chatter. Carol's mother, Jean, acted like she had known me my whole life and mentioned that she and Scotch had given me a baby gift when I was born. I knew nothing about it but thanked her anyway. Carol's younger sisters, Mary Lou, Gayle, and Linda, all at once showed up too. They had been upstairs in their bedrooms. Mary Lou and Gayle were in high school, and Linda was in junior high. They all seemed rather excited but politely subdued from time to time. The situation appeared quite odd, beyond my personal-experience-strange. I was relieved when Carol stood beside me as if she thought I would faint, have gas, or something worse. As long as I focused on Carol alone I was well; otherwise I was on the brink of psychological disaster.

Carol's mother made her mother's roast beef, baked potatoes, green beans, and a side lettuce salad for dinner. It tasted exactly like Grandma Schick's, and I was delighted that Carol's Grandma Cook and my Grandma Schick had shared recipes. Carol's home environment provided me a most comfortable dinner. The dessert was, I think, cherry pie, but whatever it was, the whole dinner was excellent and suitable for home family style in various unspeakable ways. Food helped me regather to a common focus, the wonderful old fashioned tastes of twin-like family cultures.

Amorella: It's late, orndorff. Time for bed.

Richard: I had no idea it was so late. I was right there in 1965 while writing those paragraphs above. I remember most of it like it was yesterday. I don't know what Carol wore that day, but I will never forget that secret kiss-in-a-smile at her house greeting that afternoon. The natural and most refined and wonderful kiss we had ever had happened later that night. I will never forget.

I was in a bed in a small room in the basement (does this sound familiar) when Carol knocked and came in smiling; she gave me the kiss, which I accepted readily; then she giggled, turned, and left with a cheery, "See you in the morning, Richard." It was pure class, pure Carol. I was beyond speechless. I found myself quietly weeping in pure joy and fell asleep. There was no way I would <u>not</u> ask this young woman if she would marry me.

No way. These were the most positive, memorable days I have ever had. I love her, and the memory still.

Amorella: Here is Jim Shumaker's recollection of a PA Turnpike incident. Carol needs to be up to more memory, but she recognizes the story from Fall 1966. This shows an example of how the friendship between Carol and Jim develops.

Jim: "I had graduated from Otterbein and working for FDIC. I took a class in Washington, D.C., and Carol was home in south Alexandria, Virginia, on break. I got my draft notice while there. Since I had to go back through Columbus, I asked Carol if she wanted a ride back. I picked her up at her house between Alexandria and Mt. Vernon. I was lucky I did because my license had expired, and I was unaware of it; I found out during a routine check getting on the PA Turnpike. I had insufficient cash, and banks could not cash a check to pay the fine. Carol's cash saved the day. She drove through the toll booths, and I drove the rest. After I dropped her off at Otterbein, I drove from Columbus to Colorado Springs on an expired driver's license. My recollection of the date is hazy, but probably in the Fall of 1966."

Richard: Jim's mother was a McCloy, who grew up in Westerville and went through Westerville High School like Carol's mother and my mother and father. Small town casual family connections can be crucial in unusual ways such as this.

Amorella: You have run out of words here, but I assure you that similar things always happen in families. Jim was helping Carol get back to Otterbein, and she helped him by paying his traffic fine, which he refunded her once a bank was open. One might not think an incident such as this would be remembered all these years later. Jim is eighty, and Carol is seventy-seven. You and Carol had dinner with Jim and his wife, Jeanne, at the nearby 101 Beer Kitchen on Polaris Parkway while visiting Michigan to visit family. Being dead is about friends' connections generally equal with or before family in priority.

Richard: This doesn't seem right, Amorella. I understand that relatives don't always get along, but it still doesn't seem just. Family should always come first.

Amorella: *In this book, it doesn't work that way, but then you are not dead yet, orndorff. Time will tell.*

Richard: I'm glad this dead part is fiction, if for no other reason. The stories aren't fiction, though. This work is becoming a real-life twilight zone. I always wanted to meet Rod Serling, and now I am embedding myself in a similar story.

Amorella: *The dead adjust partly because time no longer exists. The living change partially because imagination takes over. Isn't that right, Mr. Serling? – Just joking, orndorff.*

OPEN

Chapter Eleven

17 March 2023, Friday

Amorella: Most everyone has friendship stories that begin with happenstance and coincidence. These are spiritual stories to Richard because he ties them the transcendental concept of a Greater Consciousness of the Universe. One more reason he connects them with me. When Richard was five, he was told Jesus was his friend. He doesn't remember who first told him that, but later in his early teens he realized the story was self-evident. Early on Richard had a problem with this meeting with Jesus because, one, no one formally introduced him, and to Richard, so he never physically met the man. Jesus didn't even have a shadow.

This was awkwardly difficult for Richard to understand. Jesus died but he was still here. Your mother explained this to you earlier in terms of faeries. Mother said, "If you see a real faery, he will have a shadow." That made sense, but Richard never saw Jesus' shadow. Later, you learned ghosts don't have shadows. That also made sense. The only real ghost, according to elders and the Presbyterian church was the Holy Ghost. You understood the Holy Ghost to be Jesus' ghost because it made sense all the way into Junior High School. You rarely listened closely enough or talked to anyone about it because when confronting adult or child with your silly questions you became more confused to you. This was a form of self-deception because you did not ask the right questions and/or people misunderstood what you were asking about.

In junior high, Richard decided for the simplest of reasons that G-D was his friend first, and not Jesus. This was a private

thought. *People don't talk about these matters, partly because they don't know how to deal with their consciousnesses. Richard is pretending to be dead. This book is for unloading Richard's concepts, motivations, and innocence and guilt that trickle through various life experiences.*

Richard does not envision being "friends with G-D humming spiritual connection within himself first. Correct or not, this is an Understanding he has within his heartansoulanmind.

Richard: Clarification, Amorella. I Understand (with a capital) G-D exists. I sense "a Connection," but realize this connection cannot be verified. This is a very private matter of logic and reason, not faith. First, I would never expect it to be verified; and second, I can hardly imagine my Humility in such an event. I am reason oriented not faith oriented. My assumption is that I would cease to exist even as a spirit if G-D popped in, so to speak, and said, "Hello." That would be my personal conclusion. Poof. Gone. Shy-ed out, so to speak.

Amorella: All human beings are connected with the Spirit of G-D. Whether the connection is first through a human sense of a Greater Consciousness, or the link is in some mystical way connected through the Spirituality of G-D is G-D, one does not know. Richard's humility prevents him from questioning such thoughts because of arrogance in feeling such a connection might really exist. His humility warns Richard not to accidently capitalize on a 'Connection' if there ever was one. The best way to solve that would be to die on the spot.

Richard: The paragraph above makes me feel more comfortable about my sense of spirituality. I realize intellectually that an assumption of feeling a spiritual connection with the Spirit of G-D would be more than likely a rationalization dressed in spiritual garb. The only private validity I have in a reflective sense that the Spirit of G-D is near, is when I nakedly weep without humble clothes, with nothing. I am alone, hot tears running. In this, the most naked and rare of spiritual experiences, I sometimes feel like I am being wrapped in invisibility. Being then nothing, I have neither nakedness nor tears and am simply comforted in sensing I am spiritually covered and settled.

Amorella: How very orndorffian to suggest such a complete and honest thought.

The end of Richard's college days

Richard: I unofficially graduated Otterbein when I completed my student teaching at Olentangy High School in Delaware County in the Spring of 1966. I could not find a teaching job over the summer. During summer break, Carol was again working at Woodies department store in Washington.

I found a teaching job with my temporary Ohio teaching license from that following October experience because a teacher left due to her husband's transfer. I officially taught the seventh and eighth grade English and Reading programs in Magnetic Springs, a North Union Local School (Richwood, Ohio). The small two-story brick school is in Magnetic Springs, Ohio. It had students from grades one through eight. John Merriman was the principal. I thus earned my first-year Ohio retirement credit from 1966-1967. (I still communicate with John online from time to time. We are close to the same age. We both graduated from Otterbein.)

In late May 1967, I resigned from North Union County Schools and took an English teaching position at Whitehall-Yearling School District, Whitehall-Yearling High School on the east side of Columbus. A very positive, exciting time, not only professionally but because I had the financial wherewithal to ask Carol to marry.

Amorella: Richard visited Carol on 4 June 1967. The Six-Day War broke out the following day, and you were awakened by the air raid sirens going off between Alexandria and Mt. Vernon, where her parents were living. The sirens were a coincidence, but they set the tone for the day. By ten o'clock, you and Carol had readied to go to the Capitol and hear the speeches concerning the war. You saw and heard several crucial senators speak that morning.

Richard: We were right there, live, in the Gallery. Unforgettable moments.

Amorella: You had never felt so much a part of history, and here you were in the Capitol Building on such a day.

Richard: I remember that day with strong emotion and strangely, dread in the hollows of emotion.

Richard: Craig Brelsford and Alta Hibbard were married in Alta's hometown, Mansfield, Ohio, later in June 1967. I was in the wedding. That morning, I tried on the rented pants for the ceremony, they were tight, and I ripped the seam when I sat down. We rushed around until I found another pair before the wedding. More importantly, it was a bright and wonderful time, and the friendship and love between Craig and Alta still holds true, and we four are friends.

Amorella: That August before you saw Carol in Washington, you were also honored to be an usher in Fritz's marriage to Carol Moreland in Carrollton, Ohio. They moved near the campus at Ohio State University, where Fritz was enrolled in law school.

Richard: The next big event was when I asked Carol to marry me at the classy Georgetown Inn, Four Georges Restaurant in Washington, D. C. in early August 1967.

Amorella: Richard kept this proceeding a secret. The only giveaway was the location. You two never had a dinner date at such exclusive premises. Richard has forgotten what they had for conversation, drinks (other than wine), the main course, or dessert.

Richard: I remember placing my hand into my right sport coat pocket, pulling out the small white box, and quickly opening it. Carol was bemused, but smiled and slowly reached out, took the ring from the box, gently slid it on her left fourth finger, and continued smiling rather reserved and politely. Carol did not take the ring off. I paid the bill with a healthy tip. We left the restaurant for Alexandria. I don't recollect any conversation, but it was mainly essential and practical.

Amorella: Once home, everyone was excited but not as surprised as you thought they would be. Indeed, they were not as surprisingly shocked as Carol had been at the restaurant. At home, Carol was somewhat reserved and more serious-minded than usual. As you remember it, her sisters, however, were quite excited. Her parents were wonderfully supportive, but also, like Carol, more serious-minded. You were elated, orndorff, but with a sudden, strange sense of adult responsibility seeping in on the undercurrents and curtailing the merriment.

Richard: Carol and I clarified that we would wait until the following summer to get married. Things quickly grew quiet, and Carol, with her mother, headed up to Carol's bedroom to talk. The sisters promptly joined.

Dr. Hammond and I had a good, pleasant chat. We mostly conversed about my future. He said they would continue to pay Carol's tuition at Otterbein and provide her with general school expenses as they had done because that money was already accounted for. I was relieved because we felt they may no longer wish to contribute to Carol's further education as they had three more girls to put through college. I wouldn't have blamed them had they not contribute. The idea of our paying for the rest of Carol's tuition and expenses was expected in those days. Dr. Hammond was pleased that we forethought to wait until the following summer for marriage, that I would then be more established at Whitehall-Yearling High.

Amorella: Such is the life of men. Meanwhile, when the women came downstairs, it was clear what would happen. Carol's mother concurred, with Carol's blessing, that you two would be married during Thanksgiving break at the Aldersgate United Methodist Church in Alexandria, Virginia. They wanted the wedding on 25 November 1967, as it would work best with the Otterbein break and my teaching career. The date was open; the wedding was on the 25th, a Saturday evening.

Richard: I remember smiling at Carol at the announcement, but I don't think, practically speaking, Carol was all that pleased. 'Mother has spoken,' I thought. I was more enthusiastic than expected: My thought: "Good, we will legally live together. We will be husband and wife. No more charades."

Richard: In the late morning of the wedding, we men toured Arlington Cemetery. I cannot remember what we did for lunch. The women had a luncheon at the Hammond's home in Alexandria.

Amorella: The wedding took place on the evening of 25 November 1967 at the Aldersgate Methodist Church at the corners of Collingwood and Fort Hunt Roads in Alexandria, Virginia. In a formal photograph you have shown from left to right, David Short, Bob Pringle, Fritz Milligan, Richard, Scotch Hammond, Carol, Mary Lou Hammond, Jean McClintock, Cathy Orndorff, and the young, adopted Korean, Judy Reed, a perfect flower girl. A second formal photograph shows the Grandparents, from left to right: Leonard Cook, Harry Hammond, Catherine Hammond, Carol, Richard, Mae Freeman-Schick, and Clell Orndorff.

Richard: I remember the ceremony. I stumbled on a vow by almost forgetting my name. Mother gave me a dirty look. There were refreshments and dancing after. We left while people were still partying. We were returning to Westerville the next day. Our honeymoon, as such, was in a hotel in Maryland on the way to the PA Turnpike. We mostly slept in each other's arms from the day's exhaustion.

We returned to Westerville on Sunday and returned to our respective schools on Monday. Carol had a paper due for Dr.

Price's American Lit on Tuesday. Carol worked on it Monday night; she completed it Tuesday morning and turned it in. I was back in the classrooms that Monday with two Honors Freshmen, Literature and Composition classes, and three Junior classes in American Literature.

Amorella: Two years later, Carol was about to graduate from Otterbein, and this was a good time for me to resign from Whitehall-Yearling at the end of the year and go to graduate school full-time. Carol could get a job teaching her major, home economics. Within a month or so, I had two school choices, Xavier University in Cincinnati or Bowling Green State University in Bowling Green, Ohio. Bowling Green was cheaper.

No school nearby was hiring in home economics. Carol applied and took a job at Wood County Haskins Elementary School in Haskins, Ohio, not far from Bowling Green. Carol took two Otterbein summer classes to get temporary certification in elementary education. What a time. Once Carol graduated, we found a small house to rent in Bowling Green. Shortly after, we moved what we had to start a new life. She was the breadwinner, and I was on my best behavior to be a good, better-than-just-passing graduate student in education with a main focus on school system curriculum development.

Amorella: Richard had taught his Whitehall-Yearling English classes. The two teachers he remembers were a 'cousin' on the Schick side of the family, Ray Schick, the athletic director at the time; Richard thinks that Ray Schick was the reason he got the job in the first place. Richard's Department of English chairperson was Mrs. Murray. Richard taught a most enjoyable two years

with no problems in the classrooms. The first year Richard was asked to play the character Charlie Brown in a Homecoming skit where he dressed up as the cartoon character and enacted in the songfest. The only incident was during the Spring of 1969. He was attacked by an unstable junior student with an open switch-bladed knife in the hallway. Some football players down the hall saw the incident and rushed to rescue orndorff, who was attempting to put the student down without doing much physical harm. Two senior students grabbed the unstable student and pulled him away from orndorff while a third took the open switchblade from him. The boy was expelled the next day.

Richard: I was shaken up a bit. I had never been attacked with a knife before. The boy missed me with the first strike. After that, I grabbed his arm with the knife and tried to put him on the floor. He was much smaller but limber. "I was afraid if I struck him too hard with my fist, I would have beaten the shit out of him, and then, how would that look, some big guy beating a smaller high school kid to a pulp." Anyway, I was rescued, and both happy and thankful for it. I wouldn't have beaten the boy that roughly, but I was pissed off. I just hoped I would not really injure or accidentally kill the guy, even though he was the one that attacked me with an open switchblade. I began having second thoughts about a career in teaching throughout the rest of the school year.

Amorella: *Carol taught fourth grade in Northwest Ohio's less economically rural agriculturally-based Haskins, Ohio, in 1969-1970. However, the school had different problems than the city school systems like Cleveland or Cincinnati might have. The students did their work, but most needed to think beyond the high school experience and find a job to support themselves and eventually a spouse and family. Also, during certain times of*

the year, migrating child-baring families, who worked the fields when needed, stayed for a couple of months. Their children got schooling from Haskins also.

Richard: Carol had the problems most teachers have in economically-deprived schools, but the kids were primarily polite and disciplined, like Richard's junior high students had been at Magnetic Springs and, for the most part, at Whitehall-Yearling also.

Amorella: At the end of the school year, Carol did not know what Richard would be doing during the Fall of 1970. Still, she had enjoyed her first-year teaching elementary students and, more importantly, considered herself a good, well-organized, and friendly teacher, which she was and would continue to be throughout her next 33 years as a successful and professional educator.

Amorella: Richard took various graduate work at Bowling Green, mainly because he had decided early on that he did not want to be an administrator in the traditional sense of having a principalship at either a junior high or high school level.

Richard: I thought at the time that working to become a Curriculum Director at County or City School Administration Office would be a goal worth striving for because I liked books in general, and I wanted the varied specifics of high school textbooks in the fields of English, Science, History, and Government. This would hold a lifelong interest, and the pay generally is more, partly because the job is usually an eleven-month-a-year salary rather than nine months for a teacher. I would still be looking out for the individual student's best interest. It would be an exciting and fun search for the best textbooks and prices each faculty division hoped to acquire. I loved researching almost any project that I experienced from in graduate school. I love researching and writing.

Amorella: Basically, orndorff, you love learning.

Richard: You are right, Amorella. I love learning more than anything else. Life is interesting. There is always something to learn. But, of course, one can only learn when sheorhe is alive. I don't know what anyone could learn from being dead. I assume not much.

Amorella: We conclude the chapter.

OPEN

Chapter Twelve

20 March 2023, Monday

Richard: On a Thursday in late July 1970, I had a brief telephone interview with the private school superintendent, Dr. Smith of Escola Graduada de Sao Paulo, Sao Paulo, Brazil, at the Bowling Green Employment Center. Dr. Willard Smith appeared somewhat overjoyed to hear that Carol had lived overseas, that we were relatively young and had some experience teaching, that we had no children, that we were not established at any given locality other than Bowling Green, and that we were open to relocating. I was dumbfounded that he would be interested in someone with no experience traveling overseas, let alone working in a foreign country. The private American school was accredited in the United States, a plus. After the phone conversation, Carol and I had a lot of research to do before meeting with him at the Center the following afternoon.

As I had yet to find an administrative position in any school system, I was surprised that the job was not administrative but teaching English to six smaller classes, two freshmen World Literature and Composition classes, and the four senior British Literature classes. I would have never thought to apply had Carol not lived Overseas. She was more concerned with the initial and only formal interview than I was because she had a lot of field experience, so to speak, and knew what questions to ask. Dr. Smith was anxious to fill the Teacher of English position because the private school had already begun the Fall semester. A newly recruited teacher and his family had backed out at the last minute.

Carol would also have a two-year local contract (lower amount) for teaching fourth grade. We would make a total of $12,500 a year, plus we got an added supplement for renting an apartment, free lunch, and free private bus transportation from the apartment to school and back. We were also allowed to exchange the Brazilian currency for U.S. dollars to send back a poorer relative in the States. By Brazilian law, we had to agree that the money was going to a relative that needed the funds. With Bob and Patti Pringle's okay, we declared them as relatives. They were then sent the extra U.S. dollars, and they placed the check in our Westerville bank account for us. Once in Brazil, we also opened a Brazilian checking account for school deposits and local transactions.

I am, back at that time in my head. What two days it was. We each had until Monday afternoon to commit to a two-year contract; if we committed, we had to be ready to leave for Brazil within ten days or less. We would have to get State Department passports and work papers from the Brazilian consulate in Washington. We also would have to inform our families and friends, store all our stuff, and sell our one-year-old Volkswagen, but hey, we would both have a two-year teaching contract. This is so exciting to write and so much fun. It is like reliving the time. [My California cousin, Marilyn, bought the car. She was the same age as my sister Cathy. Only recently did Marilyn tell me that Grandma Schick paid for her car.]

Amorella: Remember, you are dead.

Richard: You are right, Amorella. I forgot that is what the story is about, being dead. Wow. Amazing. What a twist. I'm dead. At least it's fiction in life – but it is a reality in the Journal. Is it ironic? I don't know. I've never written about being dead before and have eleven earlier chapters on the subject. Also,

I am like Schrodinger's quantum physics cat, alive and dead simultaneously in this book. I only know how to do this project as I am currently. I will carry on, however, until I reach an unresolvable hang-up. This project is interesting, challenging, and fun for me, so why not?

Richard: According to Wikipedia, Associação Escola Graduada de São Paulo, or 'Graded', was founded in 1920, and in 1961 an elementary and high school were built on a hill overlooking Sao Paulo's suburb, Morumbi. In the 1970s, most of the classes were in English and languages in Brazilian Portuguese and French, as they still are. The school gave all graduates diplomas from either Brazilian or American high schools. Some ninety-five percent of the graduating classes enrolled in a four-year college or university within one year of graduation. then and now as I understand.

Graded is accredited by the 'Southern Association of Colleges and Schools and the Brazilian Ministry of Education, and the Association of American Schools in South America.' In addition, Graded was and is also a member of the 'U.S. National Association of Independent Schools.' The School Board was established in 1931. The classes were all college preparatory back then; however, most, like our English program, were taught as traditional Honors classes would have been in the United States.

Amorella: Enough for tonight.

Richard: I want to finish writing about our move to Brazil and the first few weeks of classes.

Amorella: *Of course, Mr. Orndorff, this sounds reasonable.*

Richard: [Suddenly and abruptly] I don't remember all this being dead.

Amorella: *You don't need to remember this as being dead. You need to reacquire it now, while you can write it down.*

Richard: Very good, Amorella. Of course, you are correct, as usual. I become too involved in the moment while writing. I don't know what to do about it.

Amorella: *That's your absorbing passion, unconscious intent, and a momentary sense of 'being alive in memory as you remember it.' You don't need to do anything but continue to use it. Don't overthink; let it work. Have a good sleep.*

Richard: You have a good sleep, too.

Amorella: *I don't sleep, orndorff.*

Richard: Have a good rest, then.

March 2023, Sunday

Amorella: *You had a McD's quarter pounder, a large diet, and two cookies from near I-71 and Polaris and are now facing north toward the birdfeeder and pine trees at Westerville's Alum Creek Park. Earlier today, you felt intensely embarrassed not* *about writing this Journal but sharing. Why? Because you are writing about yourself and not anyone else except the mentioned friends and family. How boring, you think, to ask others, friends no less, to spend time reading something you wrote.*

You are embarrassed and can be a prick about it. Now, this is the orndorff you are. You laugh self-consciously because you know it is true. But you have always been a prick about things when they suited your mood. Why is this? You can't say you are an old fart because, while true, you have always been a prick about something when being so suited.

Well, surprise, surprise. I'm going to tell you why. From my humble perspective, this is an "inborn anger" caused by the unfairness and injustice of being born human-like. What you think is akin to "original sin." That's your classification because the circumstance of the anger is inborn.

Richard: Inborn anger must come from pre-conscious, mental, or physical abnormality. There isn't even such a condition. I will research it. The first two example titles of articles from the Internet are: **1.** "Aggression Is Inborn But Worsened or Improved By One's Environment;" and **2.** "Are anger issues genetic? Can Anger run in families? – "The short answer is that anger can run in families, and genetics can play a role . . .."

Amorella: You are home realizing your physiological abnormality is in thinking on "Original Sin" first. And second, running through abnormal psychology to find an answer. First, a short definition of original sin.

Original sin - noun; Christian Theology. The tendency to sin is innate in all humans and is held to be inherited from Adam as a consequence of the Fall. The concept of original sin was developed in the writings of St. Augustine.

New Oxford English Dictionary

Richard: This is a surprise. Well, it shows I don't know much theology. I am embarrassed by the fact I somehow pushed this concept into the First Testament because the setting is in Genesis. I should know better. Very embarrassing, it is. Milton's *Paradise Lost,* that's where my mix-up on original sin is, not the Bible.

Amorella: As far as I can see, a little humility never hurt anyone.

Richard: In this last year, I discovered that my family did have a suicide on each side, one on the Schick side (one of Popo Schick's uncles in the late nineteenth century, and one suicide on Grandma Bookman-Orndorff's side, one of her half-brothers, in the early twentieth century.) From what I have gathered, I assume personal depression was the cause of both. I once thought seriously of suicide in the eighth grade and once again when I was in the mountains of Denver when I left home at nineteen. Both times, I attribute this to depression, not anger. I never attempted suicide. It was not a reasonable probability because it would not help me solve my own problems.

Amorella: Back to your original sense of "inborn anger" earlier in today's daily journal, you commented that it was your opinion that the inborn anger was "caused by the unfairness and injustice of being born human-like." Richard: I agree that in my conscious life, even as early as three to five, I had a small grasp of unfairness and injustice in the world. One example is mentioned in Chapter One when, with my Grandfather Orndorff, I met his neighbor, Mr. Press Reynolds, who had been born a slave. So, I partially understood the sense of injustice. And, another example, when FDR died, I understood more, not entirely, of course, the concept of unfairness in the world – WWII – concentration camps – civil rights.

Richard: Reinforcement of the anger continued throughout my public schooling and beyond. This is not inborn anger. Besides, before I was born, how could I realize that as a tiny undeveloped Preemie, was human-like?

I had an understanding – I felt a sixth sense or an inference that I did not want to be born, that I had a choice. Strangely, it implies I sensed I had been somewhere else consciously before birth. Perhaps, the 'somewhere else' was caused by my sense of being in the womb as an individual, thus, confusing this with a later concept of free will. Other than that, I have no probable idea.

Amorella: My perspective is that your human spirit, a combined heartanmind, and one soul, is where two souls were originally. In those days and until recently, you intuitively felt I, the Amorella, was an Angel of G-D. What else? Not G-D, certainly. Even recently, in this book, you readily accept the concept of the Spirit of G-D because of humility more than anything else. You get this without realizing that your idea of the Spirit of G-D is through reasoning, not faith.

Richard: I would have never consciously come to your 'reasoning' conclusion here. This is exhausting to me spiritually, Amorella. I wonder if Angels exist. I capitalize the word, though, even with substantial doubts. I also have smaller hesitations that tell me to respect the concept of an Angel existing by capitalizing the word. The capital letter is entirely meaningful to me in my heartansoulanmind.

Amorella: This, you see, is where I exist, in your heartansoulanmind, in the immortal part with no physics. That's how it is.

Richard: Even if this were so, in real life, Amorella, I would only capitalize 'heartansoulanmind if standard grammar calls for it. There is a sacred principle here, a Higher Standard.

Amorella: What if, after you are dead and gone, someone decided to capitalize heartansoulanmind anyway, as a reinforcer, that you were someone special, when you saw yourself as a mostly misunderstanding though otherwise regular ordinary heartansoulanmind?

Richard: If it could be proven to me that someone did this, no matter how good herorhis intentions were, I would forgive this person of human error, the same kind of error anyone might make in herorhis lifetime. I would forgive because I would have no choice as a human spirit. Otherwise, this error would become my burden, which it clearly is not. Pause. This appears to be a hypothetical or theoretical lesson in ethics and even politeness, Amorella. Is that the point?

Amorella: Are you surprised at your response?

Richard: No, it didn't take that long to realize that for a very selfish and reasonable reason, I was not to blame for something someone else did because sheorhe thought it was in the best thing for 'the cause,' whatever that cause happened to be at the time. For example, this person trying to help might think: 'Here, let's capitalize his heartansoulanmind, so it reinforces the message. No harm in that, as far as I can see.'

Holy shit, Amorella. How far, in the sentence above, can this woman or man *see*? No one can know what herorhis lifetime was/is about other than surviving and attempting to do something honorable and worthwhile for oneself and for the human species in the process of living what hopefully is a good life.

And, in conjunction with living well and taking special care of the environment and wherewithal of most all living things on the planet that help nurture a good, respectful, and healthy attitude, what more can a person want or need in a broader line of thinking positive about humankind? And, of course, in allowing the nurture of human friendship when and where it is mutually acceptable to one another. I don't have anything more to say on this subject.

Amorella: *Good. This concludes the chapter.*

OPEN

Chapter Thirteen

22 March 2023, Friday

Richard: I remember leaving for Brazil from the Columbus, Ohio airport. A few friends and family were there to see us off. I found everything about the plane we were on to New York JFK Airport interesting because it was a new experience. It was one more plane ride for Carol, but it was to a new continent and country to live and explore. The only other continent was Antarctica; at least, that is what I thought. How would I ever catch up with Carol's travel and living experiences? I wasn't, but this was a new beginning regarding travel. If I remember right, we took an afternoon Delta flight to JFK, and we would then take a Pan Am night flight for a morning arrival at Rio de Janeiro and then take the now-defunct Varig Airline from Rio to Sao Paulo.

Amorella: I am interrupting here because you immediately said to yourself after reading this online, "Now, isn't that strange? All this time, you thought Varig was still an airline; it was until 2006. Then, the passenger service went bankrupt, and its cargo service also went bankrupt in 2012. No more Varig, according to Wikipedia.

Richard: I held a factual reality that has yet to exist since 2006. This means something, but I don't know how to explain it. What do dead people's spirits do when they find what they thought were facts even though their lifetimes were no longer even while they were alive? This is quite bizarre to consider. What other pieces of information do I have in my head that are no longer true? One might ask, "It doesn't make any difference, does it orndorff?" However, that is not true, it does make a difference, or it can make a difference if happenstance allows it.

Amorella: What kind of happenstance, Mr. Orndorff?

19 March 2023, Sunday

Richard: I am thinking about the happenstance from Friday, the last entry in the daily journal about not knowing that Varig Airlines no longer exists, and Carol and I believe the airline was still in business. This is not the same, but it is close because we thought Kim, Paul, and the boys were involved in soccer matches this weekend. We discussed this at the kitchen table with Craig and Alta last night on the assumption they were in Michigan when they were not. Why, then, on philosophical subjects, are any of the hypotheses and/or theories assumed true. At the same time, some may be true from a human being's perspective but not accurate and undoubtedly not True with a capital. The truth will make you free. What, then, is this Truth with a capital?

Oddly, perhaps, but from my present perspective, "G-D exists" is the only Truth I can honestly understand to have the capital 'T'. . Some people suggest the universe we exist in is an illusion or a dream, but the universe is a truth without a capital, which in my mind is closer to the truth than the universe is an illusion or a dream. From a human perspective, if the universe (and us in it) is an illusion, then we don't exist. But scientifically, we do exist. And, if the universe is a dream, where is the verification for that?

dream - noun

1 a series of thoughts, images, and sensations occurring in a person's mind during sleep: I had a recurrent dream about falling from great heights.

- [in singular] a state of mind in which someone is or seems unaware of their immediate surroundings: he had been walking around in a dream all day.

2 a cherished aspiration, ambition, or ideal: I fulfilled a childhood dream when I became champion | the girl of my dreams | [as modifier]: they'd found their dream home.

- an unrealistic or self-deluding fantasy: maybe he could get a job and earn money—but he knew this was just a dream.

- a person or thing perceived as wonderful or perfect: her new man's an absolute dream | it was a dream of a backhand | she's a couturier's dream

New Oxford American Dictionary

Richard: If the universe is a dream, the vision has exhausted its original meaning. And, the hypothesis that we and the universe are a part of G-D's dream is anthropomorphic: "treating animals, gods, or objects as if they are human in appearance, character, and behavior." - **Cambridge Dictionary**.

Amorella: While you are at it, orndorff, G-D, as used in this work, is not a noun even with a capital N or NOUN. The hyphen suggests the letters are not even a word, and to say G-D is but a concept is demeaning. That is my perspective for those with an individual and/or a collective sense of G-D. Why are some human minds so small-like? Grow spiritually. You are free to do so. If you do not choose to mature spiritually, rudeness will continue to awaken within.

Richard: I did not see the above paragraph appearing in my mind. 'Rudeness' is a strange word to place in such a context. Pause. I would never choose such a word; however, considering what I observed below, especially from Wikipedia, it is a good word to use in this context. Amazing, who would have ever thought I would write such.

rudeness - noun 1 lack of manners; discourtesy: I will not tolerate rudeness | Alice becomes disgusted by the rudeness of her three companions. 2 dated roughness or simplicity.

New Oxford American Dictionary

Richard: I spent the last half hour looking for the Graded yearbooks. I found *Aquilla*, 1971, our first year, which ought to be enough for recollections. This yearbook needs to be included; the *Aquilla* 1972 is somewhere here. This, the 1971 yearbook, is dedicated to one of my favorite people: Mr. Vladimir Rodionoff, math teacher extraordinaire. A Russian who had spent time in Soviet prison. He majored in Chinese philosophy in Russia and later taught at Columbia University during the Summer break (our Winter). Unfortunately, the United States denied him citizenship. Vlad went to Brazil instead and became a Brazilian chess champion who played Spassky. He spoke Russian, English, German, and Brazilian Portuguese. Vlad was a significant contributor to my life experience. Vlad's quote for this *Aquilla* yearbook is:

"We are the music makers, and we are the dreamers of dreams."

The other major contributor to my life was Mr. Roger Allain, a French teacher. These are my recollections. Roger had spent twenty years with his English wife and their family in a 'Friends' Commune in Paraguay. They lived life to their ideals. They left England/France in the 1930s, as I remember it. Roger and his wife had twelve children, and none continued in the communal life as adults. Roger and his wife left for Brazil, where he taught French, his native language. Roger spoke excellent English, German, Spanish, and Brazilian Portuguese. Roger taught me how to walk alone in the Rain Forest and live my philosophy of life the best I can. Roger's quotation for the Aquilla yearbook is from Keats:

A thing of beauty is a joy forever

Its loveliness increases; it will never

Pass into nothingness, but still will

Keep a bower quiet for us, and a sleep

Full of dreams, and health,

And quiet breathing.

Vlad and Roger were kind and gentle men. They were my friends and teachers for two years. I will never forget it either. Why? They became free enough to live good and philosophical lives as they wished in a world not easily constructed for such private settings and solutions. Of course, compromises must be made in this world, but their struggles to fully live good moral, and ethical lives make them heroes in my book. Tears rise to my eyes as I write. Enough on these two. May I eventually visit them in the timeless spiritual world beyond.

OPEN

Chapter Fourteen

25 March 2023, Saturday

Richard: This is the first day of Spring. I woke up thinking about the essentials of surviving lost in the rain forest. Yesterday, I could not remember a thing. This morning I remember that a spoon can be more essential than a knife. I remember because I would have never thought of carrying a spoon. Roger would have laughed to read this. The twinkle and wit in his eye. I can see them yet.

Amorella: The most crucial point in the above paragraph is "The twinkle and wit in his eye."

Richard: What a simple revelation, Amorella. I am blessed to know you. What a good teaching on what is more important than surviving lost in the rainforest, especially since I am as already dead.

Amorella: Your thoughts are more helpful if you remember that you are physically dead in this part of the book.

Richard: Being dead is an essential dimension in this story.

Amorella: Spiritual survival is not in a dimension.

Richard: It all appears the same to me, a dimension, a place in space, whatever. It is early for speculation.

Amorella: *Spiritual surviving is as a fold in a fluffy pillow.*

Richard: Another time, Amorella. I'm tired.

Amorella: *You returned to bed, fell into a light sleep, then had a vision of how the fellow human spirits would appear to you as a spirit yourself. It is good that you put it down here as it is in your original phone notes. You do not have the time the notes began, but you have the concluding time. This began at about six o'clock or a little earlier.*

The Note: The sketch of shades in gray - faces/upper bodies, but I saw no hands - an appearance than a fading, in parts and whole. Clothing of choice / no colors / facial details clear and sharp with water liquid shimmer on eyes / facial and head hair apparent / With hints of moisture in the atmospheric setting /

Faces independent with their own free will and reflection of own personality – this is similar to how I saw people under hypnosis in the 1980s, projected, by me, back when I was in incubation, I saw nurses and people with no hands or fingers. A flash of eye, lid, and lash – spirit images

*[**Amorella:** You modified the above slightly for clarification.]*

Richard: This early morning note took at least twenty minutes to write. There is not much in the notes, not nearly as much as I was taking at the time. This is embarrassing now, but it

appeared genuine to me then. A slightly moving sketch of a man's face is how it was drawn in my mind first. This shows me that the above was more of an active imagination than an actual vision.

Amorella: *Why do you write, "This above was more of an active imagination than an actual vision," orndorff?*

Richard: I cannot imagine this event happening in any other way than through imagination. 'Fractal fiction' that is what it is. That is how I am letting it go. - rho

Amorella: *Cats were fed, and you have been a 'lapping place' for Jadah for twenty minutes or so while listening to pleasant piano on Pandora. Blue skies at present, and it is cool and crisp outside. Spring Equinox begins around five this afternoon, according to the Dispatch. You may want to know where to start with this chapter regarding this Journal.*

Flashbacks on living in Brazil

Richard: I am because I need to figure out what is relevant. I can't remember anyone or any Brazil Events other than when Craig, Alta, and Jim visited during Christmas vacation that first year. We were on Summer break, and they took as much time as possible from their Christmas vacations. Craig was a history teacher; Alta, a social worker, and Jim, who earned a Purple Heart, during his time in Vietnam, had returned to the FDIC.

Carol and I took trips within Brazil, but they were mostly travel and explore journeys, some being high school senior class trips as chaperons each year. Outside Brazil, we visited Argentina, Uruguay, Bolivia, and Peru, each memorable, but nothing I remember influenced me to the core, like Roger Allain and Vlad Rodionoff.

I had memorable students also. Over the years, in all my classes, I had notable students. Some I grew to love as my own nieces or nephews, and very few I would have adopted to raise had the need been there. I loved my students, I attempted to treat them as an individual, and part of the inner joy of teaching was watching students grow and mature as young adults. My classes were always set in my mind as college sophomore British literature, world literature, or American literature classes. Those were my high-level college sophomore. My freshmen class was taught like a college freshman class as much as appropriate. Freshmen and sophomores were treated much like high school seniors regarding classroom atmosphere (politeness and decorum). Higher expectations and higher standards. The students did not know this, and it only sometimes worked. Sometimes a freshman or sophomore class had to be treated like they were still in junior high, but those were rare in decades of teaching literature and composition.

Amorella: While we are on the subject, what about those students you could not reach?

Richard: That's a good question, Amorella. The basic answer is that I let them be. I tolerated them and hoped they would accept me. I hoped and requested that another teacher or counselor might come to their rescue. That, I found, was usually the case, another teacher of any subject, a coach/teacher of a guidance counselor. Occasionally, a nurse, custodian, assistant principal, or principal fit in the role of teacher/counselor for a student. Sometimes, no one could help.

Amorella: Do you, or did you ever feel any guilt for any relationship with a student?

Richard: No. I became close to one of my male students because I could have adopted him if he needed to adopted. He graduated and moved on. I still hear from him from time to time, always by email. I had one female student that I would have adopted. My feelings for her were similar to those for our own daughter. She also moved on. I still remember her too. I don't know why I felt so deeply about some students. I also had a heartfelt closeness with a few others, male and female. In all, I was in love most with the maturing nature of their minds. Those females who were quite attractive I shied from for professional reasons. I put those young ladies in a personal category of being adopted nieces; that was enough separation in my mind.

Amorella: You have been honest, orndorff. I would have let you know if you were not. Human emotions are complex. It is sometimes difficult to see the forest for the trees. In cases with humans, some of those forests appearing to be trees are nothing more than taller bushes being seen from being up too close, like the observation from your Lanai: the bushes in your short backyard and the more towering trees yards beyond.

Amorella: Spiritual survival is not in a dimension. What do you say to that as a statement?

Richard: It all appears the same to me, a dimension, a place without time and space.

Amorella: *Spiritual survival is as a fold in a fluffy pillow.*

Richard: Surviving is as a fold without time and space?

Amorella: *Yes.*

Richard: I need to look this up. Amorella, please underline the relevant selections.

fold - noun 1 a form or shape produced by the gentle draping of a loose, full garment or piece of cloth: the fabric fell in soft folds.

• an area of skin that sags or hangs loosely.

2 mainly British an undulation or gentle curve of the ground; a slight hill or hollow: the house lay in a fold of the hills.

• Geology a bend or curvature of strata.

3 A line or crease produced in paper or cloth as the result of folding it.

• a piece of paper or cloth that has been folded: a fold of paper slipped out of the diary.

fold2 noun a[n] pen or enclosure in a field where livestock, mainly sheep, can be kept.

• (the fold) a group or community, especially when perceived as the locus of a particular set of aims and values: he's performing a ritual to be accepted into the fold.

-fold - suffix 1 in an amount multiplied by: threefold.

2 consisting of so many parts or facets: twofold.

New Oxford English American Dictionary

FOLD: List of definitions relative to Amorella's importance of the word.

1. a group or community, especially when perceived as the locus of a particular set of aims and values;

2. consisting of so many parts or facets: twofold.

3. a line or crease produced

4. a form or shape produced by the gentle draping

5. geology - a bend or curvature of strata

6. an enclosure

Richard: I also need to look up spiritual.

spiritual - adjective - **1** relating to or affecting the human spirit or soul instead of material or physical things: I'm responsible for his spiritual welfare | the spiritual values of life.

• (of a person) not concerned with material values or pursuits.

2 relating to religion or religious belief: the tribe's spiritual leader.

Spirit - noun - **1** is the nonphysical part of a person, which is the seat of emotions and character; the soul: we seek a harmony between body and spirit.

- the nonphysical part of a person regarded as their true self and capable of surviving physical death or separation: a year after he left, his spirit is still present.

- the nonphysical part of a person manifested as an apparition after their death; a ghost: a priest performed a rite of exorcism, and the wandering spirit was ousted.

- a supernatural being: shrines to nature spirits.

- (the Spirit) the Holy Spirit

Spirit 2 [in singular] those qualities regarded as forming the definitive or typical elements in the character of a person, nation, or group or in the thought and attitudes of a particular period: the university symbolizes the nation's egalitarian spirit.

- [with adjective] [any] person identified with their most prominent mental or [and] moral characteristics or with their role in a group or movement: he was a leading spirit in the conference.

- a specified emotion or mood, especially one prevailing at a particular time: I hope the team will build on this spirit of confidence.

- (spirits) a person's mood: My spirits were low as I sat alone in that corridor.

- the attitude or intentions with which someone undertakes or regards something: he confessed in a spirit of self-respect, not defiance.

- the quality of courage, energy, and determination or assertiveness: his visitors admired his spirit and good temper.

- the actual meaning or the intention behind something as opposed to its strict verbal interpretation: the rule had been broken in spirit if not in letter.

3 (usually spirits), mainly British strong distilled liquor such as brandy, whiskey, gin, or rum.

- [mass noun, with modifier] a volatile liquid, especially a fuel, prepared by distillation: aviation spirit.

- **archaic** is a solution of volatile components extracted from something, typically by distillation or by solution in alcohol: spirits of turpentine. Archaic is a highly refined substance or fluid thought to govern vital phenomena.

New Oxford English American Dictionary

Richard: Amorella, please, for consistency, add italics below to the relevant words in the above definition.

1. *relating to or affecting the human spirit*

2. *the nonphysical part of a person, which is the seat of emotions and character;*

3. *[any] person identified with their most prominent mental [and] moral characteristics*

4. *the attitude or intentions with which someone undertakes or regards something*

5. *the quality of courage and determination*

6. *the actual meaning or the intention behind something*

7. *a solution of volatile components extracted from something*

8. *a highly refined thought to govern vital phenomena.*

Richard: Here is a summary of spiritual and fold in this book, which are based on the **New Oxford American Dictionary.**

SPIRITUAL: The nonphysical part of a person which is the seat of emotions and character [which is] a highly refined thought to govern vital phenomena. A person identified with their most prominent mental [and] moral characteristics [with] a solution of volatile components extracted the attitude or intentions with which someone undertakes or regards, the real meaning or the intent behind the quality of courage and determination relating to or affecting the human spirit.

FOLD: A group or community, especially when perceived as the focus of a particular set of aims and values, consisting of many parts or facets. These parts or facets mold as a line or crease, allowing gentle draping to produce a form or shape. This bend or curvature of the strata creates an enclosure for the group or community.

Surviving - adjective - remaining alive, especially after the death of another or others: there were no surviving relatives.

- continuing to exist; remaining intact: surviving correspondence alludes to his aristocratic lifestyle.

Survive verb [no object] continues to live or exist, especially despite danger or hardship: against all odds, the child survived.

- [with object] continue to live or exist in spite of (an accident or ordeal): he has survived several assassination attempts.

- [with object] remain alive after the death of (a particular person): he was survived by his wife and six children.,

- [no object] managed to keep going in difficult circumstances: she had to work day and night and survive on two hours' sleep.

Richard: Now what, Amorella?

Amorella: These four definitions are relevant.

surviving adjective

1. remaining alive, especially after the death of another or others: there were no surviving relatives.

2. continuing to exist; remaining intact: surviving correspondence alludes to his aristocratic lifestyle.

survive verb [no object]

1. continue to exist, especially despite danger or hardship:

2. continue to exist despite an accident or ordeal

Richard: This is interesting, Amorella. The vibe: **1.** I'm picking up that even though a person's heartansoulanmind survives death, **2.** obstacles can lead to one's non-existence as a human spirit.

*Amorella: **This is the Rule**. If a heartansoulanmind cannot eventually find a way to forgive herorhimself for herorhis supposed sins, sheorhe cannot consciously forgive others. Every heartansoulanmind also must be willing to forgive everyone else's supposed human sins; this is for the common eternal survival of every heartansoulanmind within the Fold. This is not punishment. This is for the growth and maturity of the individual heartansoulanmind within the continuing human heartansoulanmind community.*

Richard: Although I readily understand its function, this does not appear to be an easy task,

Amorella: Existence in any form is not for the weak-hearted.

Richard: I thank my lucky stars. This work is a realistic simulation; that I am not physically dead.

Amorella: *If you do not wish to continue this book, it is your choice, Mr. Orndorff. In this work, anyone, living or physically dead, always has free will.*

Richard: The "lucky stars" comment was an automatic response. If this is a realistic portrayal of how the heartansoulanmind can survive physical death, so be it.

Amorella: *This concludes the chapter; or not?*

Richard: Who would have thought? I find myself using this phrase at the end of the chapters. How can I not consciously know or realize surprises such as this? No one said anything about a Rule. And, only one rule, for that matter. The real kicker for me is Amorella's comment: Existence in any form is not for the weak-hearted. I feel dumbfounded, then I mumble out loud, "What the hell, Amorella?"

Amorella: *You remain an honest man, orndorff.*

Richard: "I'll be damned."

Amorella: *You're a funny man.*

Addendum

26 March 2023, Sunday, early morning

Richard: The irony and the dark humor in Chapter Fourteen are unbelievable.

Amorella: Good morning, Mr. Orndorff.

Richard: I don't know what else to say, Amorella.

Amorella: Are you going to continue with this book?

Richard: I wholeheartedly accept this work as honestly written.

Amorella: That is a wise choice, orndorff. Good for you.

Richard: I can't help myself; it is the exponent of dark humor that keeps me writing. If this were a realistic portrayal of spiritual life after death, the dark humor would not be so dark.

Amorella: Humor saves your first full day of Spring.

Richard: I cannot understand why I wrote, "The dark humor would not be so dark after all." In all honesty, though, that is what came to mind.

Amorella: This is because you have just come to an Understanding with the Capital. This then is the conclusion of the chapter.

OPEN

Chapter Fifteen

28 March 2023, Tuesday

Amorella: Doug sent you a note after your note to him about remembering the crosses above the church one night in 1959, when you were driving about looking at the stars and talking and hoping to spot a UFO.

Dick, I wish we had seen a UFO. The crosses were unexpected. You sometimes remind me of Job of the Old Testament with your discussion about apologizing to G-D. Keep writing your Journal.

Have a nice day!

Doug

Amorella: It is heartening to me, old man, that you two found each other again after all these years. You have very similar spiritual, scientific, and UFO interests, which you have always had. I'll call you 'Brothers of a Rare Kind.'

Richard: Speaking of UFOs, I have a new version of *Diplomat's Pouch*, a novel I was going to publish a few years ago. The only two Readers were Doug and Fritz.

Amorella: This takes courage for Richard. I stopped him from going further. I am providing an explanation because, to the

Reader, it might appear he is trying to plug a book he did not dare to self-publish. He was terrified to publish the work because he felt it might be completely misunderstood. The man is a misplaced recluse. He has a few special people who have said they like his stories, a hand's worth at most.

Richard: I love you, Amorella because you get right to the point. I don't trust people in general. Everybody has a self-interest, including me. I am an old man, but I am not tired of living. I like to be left alone to do what I want, which, ironically, is mostly nothing but thinking, creating with reason and imagination, and writing. I have everything I need, family and good friends.

Amorella: The above paragraph is a prime example of his thinking on this subject. He is a recluse. The only example he can think of is Jonathon Swift, the eighteenth-century writer, but then it sounds like Richard wants to be famous like Jonathon Swift. What an ego, you, the Reader, might think, but the man deep down has little ego left in him, if he ever really had much, to begin with. I am embarrassing him terribly.

Richard: I have nothing to say on this subject, Amorella.

Amorella: I will end this by adding the concluding paragraph of Richard's unpublished Diplomat's Pouch. For reference, oSoul is one of the characters in the novel. She is the soul of a hybrid alien. Another character is Diplomat Burroughs, who is a hybrid strain of both human and marsupial human DNA. Within the story, this is from an accident with another intent in a lab. The Diplomat appears female enough, but she has a uterus, a pouch, and no breasts. This is Diplomat's soul speaking the last words in the unpublished book, Diplomat's Pouch. The slight additions below are for additional clarity.

> **oSoul.** If you were to read Richard's Working Notes on this earlier book, you would see a notation that Amorella suggests to Richard. *"It is time to view this book as a transcendental philosophy similar to that of American writer, Ralph Waldo Emerson, and other writers of the British Isles and Europe."* **Amorella will use the story format for a higher purpose; to show Mr. Orndorff's conscious spiritual transition from being an agnostic.**

Amorella: This transition began when he was a Freshman and read "Rime of the Ancient Mariner" by Samuel Taylor Coleridge in Miss Florence Harley's English class at Westerville High School located at State and Park in Westerville. This work, a classroom project, was the seed that sparked his heartansoulanmind into the concept of 'transcendentalism' Reading Ralph Waldo Emerson's Essays allowed Richard to grow.

Later, Dr. John Coulter, when teaching World Literature at Otterbein University, introduced Richard to Immanuel Kant, which helped the concept of transcendentalism flourish in his mind during the early and mid-1960s. This was when Mr. Orndorff attached his heartansoulanmind to the Beatnik literary and social movement.

Transcendentalism took on a more practical orientation when he worked at Blendon Township as a summer caretaker at Blendon Township Cemetery while in college. He transferred to Westerville City for summer work and eventually became a summer caretaker and gravedigger at Otterbein Cemetery at the corner of Knox and Walnut.

This story, Diplomat's Pouch, began in an open grave that Richard finished digging and laid down in to rest in the coolness on a hot day. He fell asleep for a time and had an unconscious dream about receiving a diplomatic-like pouch before awakening and climbing out from the earth's shade into hot sunlight.

Richard and his wife, Carol's relatives, are buried at Otterbein Cemetery just as he and Carol will be buried there. Their headstone is already in place. Richard has rested and slept in an open grave, digging in this hallowed burial ground. Mr. Orndorff will not climb out of a grave this next time.

- The End -

Amorella: The above is from the conclusion of the unpublished Diplomat's Pouch by Richard H. Orndorff. The book's contents were partially edited and selected from the previously published material in 2006, 2007, and 2008.

Richard: Fair enough, Amorella. Thank you.

Amorella: Let's return to Brazil during that first year, 1970-1971.

Richard: The last Brazilian sequence was in Chapter Fourteen. We had been talking to our neighbors in the apartment building, K. and G. during September; then, I moved to the event on the public bus and how good the Paulistanos were to Carol and me while attempting to leave the packed bus during rush hour.

Amorella: *What other events do you remember with your Brazilian friends, K. and G.?*

Richard: We practiced our Portuguese and helped them understand how living in the United States might be for them. We told them we could easily understand them when they spoke English and that they would do well in adjusting to living in the United States for a year or two.

The school year

As we entered our school year, the focus mainly was teaching our students and learning more about how our private school system worked. As I knew in high school, everyone stuck to their schedules and lesson plans. We did look out for student drug use, but day-to-day, it did not play any real role. Carol and I quickly adjusted to the routines while moving into the school year.

I could do more experimental teaching with Freshmen. This was easier because of the diversity of literature and poetry. We read Orwell's *1984* and Huxley's *Brave New World* and *Animal Farm*. I developed an independent learning packet on propaganda, what it was, and how to spot it. This was fed from reading and discussing the three books. Propaganda is something I felt the Freshmen needed to have as a background. No one in the administration or faculty objected.

I realized Roger Allain, the French teacher, knew much more about English and world literature than I did. In fact, more than once, when I asked, he would point out what was more relevant in my teaching and lecture notes. He was older and had much broader experiences in world literature and history. I learned some aspects of English literature and literature that I could have only learned from someone with a vast background built within a European structured educational system. I am very grateful for that.

We did go on a few shorter trips and local adventures with Larry and Darla S. They were in their thirties and had a daughter in upper elementary. They lived a few blocks south of us in Santo Amora. Larry was from Arizona and taught English and drama. Darla, his wife, worked as a substitute teacher. We got along well and made good company for one another during our stay in Brazil. Once we returned to the States, we went our separate ways. Carol and I immensely enjoyed our fellow faculty members at Graded; they were diverse individuals with a common goal of being good teachers for the students.

Amorella: How were things different in your second year?

Richard: I was given Department Chair by Carol W., who taught English, but because of Jim W., her husband's business interests, she was hired for a longer than two-year contract, and as such, she, for a good reason, was chosen head of the department for continuity. Carol and I became closer friends partly because she attended Miami University in Oxford while I did my graduate work at Bowling Green State University. We were both familiar with Ohio and its educational systems.

Carol W. and her husband, Jim, had two daughters, R. and V. I had them both for English literature, R. in my first year and V. in my second. The W. family and we were both Sao Paulo's British Club members. Carol and Jim took Carol and me sailing in their lightning class sailboat near the nearby Santo Amaro British

Club. Carol W. and her family were very kind to us. We kept in contact for a year or two after we returned to the United States.

I was also selected to be one of two teachers to sit in on the Board of Directors meetings as a way for the high school faculty that second year. Teachers were never allowed to attend a Board of Directors meeting before this. Bob Fumo. was selected to represent the elementary school. We were to give some input into the Board's directives and rules. This was a first for Escola Graduada do Sao Paulo. I felt honored to speak for and collect information for the high school faculty. Bob and I had regular private conversations after each meeting. Being in those meetings was a very unique experience. I had had no background with a private school board before, nor have I since.

29 March 2023, Wednesday

Amorella: Jadah is curled and sleeping contentedly in the jungle leaf-printed chair in the Lanai; Spooky is elsewhere. The sky appears blue primarily with light-weighted silk cloth-o-cloud as a robed dressing. The birds are having at the tube of light brownish grain hanging on the little hook of black aluminum poles into the ground. They go straight up and down as poles like a line of perpendicularly thick horizontal thought.

Richard: That's a mouthful of word-making, Amorella.

Amorella: You have a pink-papered list of professional comrades at Escola Graduada you would like to include due to your fortune of still living. You cannot choose how deep gratitude you have for personally knowing and working with them, as it would be like selecting friends from a lineup. Mary Ann B., who taught shorthand and typing, is one to include.

You still chat with her Brazilian/American husband, Tito, who worked at Graded then. He was a kind, inquisitive young fellow who later earned his education at the University of Sao Paulo and his doctorate and a professorship at a university in Florida.

In recent times, Bob Fumo, Tito and you communicated via email about politics during Trump's time in office. Tito lives with his wife along the east Florida coast.

Richard: I forgot Tito's name once or twice. Not remembering Carol and Kimberly, wife and daughter, is also embarrassing. I have forgotten other good friends' names from time to time too. I don't feel embarrassed about forgetting my name, though.

Amorella: You don't feel your own name counts, orndorff, and in here, it doesn't because you are dead and don't have official legal ownership of it any longer. In that quirky sense, you are ahead of the game.

Richard: Pirate Dick sounds like a good name if I'm one up on names. Pirate Dick has a good ring to it as Dick has a couple meanings of its own. This is a little thought, so Little Dick will do too. Little Dick, the Pirate. Amorella, what about the other names on my list?

Amorella: Mary Ann R. was a teacher of English like yourself; you once took a professional trip to the American school in Rio with her. She was both kind and direct. That's what you remember most. You liked and enjoyed working with her and everyone else.

Richard: Indeed, that is true. We got along well. Her boyfriend was a pilot for a Brazilian airline if I remember correctly.

Amorella: Diane C. was another English teacher in the department. She was helpful to you in the early days, as was Katharine T. in Guidance. Other comrades in education were Eduardo P. and Roger M., both math teachers; the science teacher, Elizabeth P.; and the Physical Education teacher, a Canadian, Vern P. There are a couple more, particularly new teachers from your second year at Graded. Do not concern yourself – another sleight-of-hand secret from Beyond is the surprise. When a former acquaintance drifts nearby, you recognize one another and stop for a chat.

In this book, any friendship and even neighborliness may be mutually recognized; the sense of this is as a blessing-in-disguise for both. Who needs harps and trumpets? This is a peek of what heaven is like.

Richard: I am overwhelmed, Amorella. Such a thought I would have never expected to read. There are those people in life forgotten today, but if I were to meet again, it would bring tears of sudden joy to my old eyes. A simple unrestrained grin and a "How are you?" would do as a starter. I am blown away with this thought, simply blown away. To me, this is what heavenly joy is all about. What a spontaneous wish.

Richard: The end of the second school year came quickly. The school helped us sell our furniture and make sure our debts, finances, and professional status were for transfer back to the States. It was amazing how easily this flowed, right up to a taxi

173

to the airport. Once we lifted off, it was a long journey traveling home. We were carrying a lot of mixed feelings and our luggage – we were sad about leaving our friends, the school, the city, and the country. At the same time, happy to be returning home to see family and friends. Beyond that, in a conventional sense, we were in the private joy of securing employment before we left.

We never returned for a visit, but then, that lifetime vanished. The Sao Paulo of today looks a little like it did when we were there in the early seventies. Most of the student's parents are dead, and the faculty we knew are now quite old or have passed. Some of our dear students have not survived either. Our only return connections which are through memory, writings, photographs, high school yearbooks, and sometimes Facebook.

Amorella: After returning from flights from Sao Paul to Rio, Rio to Miami, and Miami to Columbus, you stayed with Grandma Schick, and you borrowed David Short's old gray Plymouth for a week or two for necessary transportation.

You drove Carol to the Cincinnati area from Columbus. You visited the small brick Indian Hill administration building where you signed the contract and were contacted by Mr. S., an assistant principal at Indian Hill High School.

Within the day of meeting Mr. S., he found you a two-bedroom apartment on Montgomery Road in Silverton, Ohio. The apartment was on the second floor of an older 1930s two-story brick building. Montgomery Road, the 3-C Highway, is one of the old arteries through downtown Cincinnati.

Richard: Up on Montgomery Road, a mile or so from our apartment, was a small shopping center called Kenwood Plaza. The Kenwood area is in the Indian Hill Exempted Village public schools. North of Kenwood along Montgomery Road is the suburb of Montgomery, which has Indian Hill schools to its east.

Amorella: You obviously needed two cars and bought new VWs, green and yellow, on timed payments at the Montgomery VW dealer. You remember the U.S. VWs looked more cosmopolitan than those in Brazil, mainly because they came with attached bells, whistles, and better paint, but not better actual leather seats. As a result, the cars appeared to you as showcased VWs rather than those VWs presented as more utilitarian-like in Brazil.

Amorella: Carol's elementary school was in Wyoming, a city suburb and home of Procter & Gamble, among other prominent businesses about eight miles west of Kenwood. Nearby, Montgomery's Sycamore Public Schools had high graduation ratings, with a significant percentage of their students continuing their education at a nearby college or university.

After Carol earned her Master's in Education from the University of Cincinnati through part-time effort. She took employment in Sycamore Public Schools, teaching fourth-grade students at Blue Ash Elementary. Carol finished her thirty-two-year Ohio teaching career at Blue Ash in 2004. I give praise for her teaching style and dedication. Carol exemplified a model professional teacher throughout her career.

Richard: Thank you very much, Amorella. I will tell her so.

Amorella: You were a good teacher, orndorff, but hardly one to model.

Richard: I'm forever pinned with your understandable and quite justified point, Amorella. Carol was a better and more professional teacher than I was. I am proud of my friend, partner, and wife, Carol, my love.

OPEN

Chapter Sixteen

31 March 2023, Saturday

Amorella: You woke up thinking about John Douglas Goss and how he was the first to be in your Closest Friends category. By your way of thinking, your closest friends in order by the age of friendship are Doug, from third/fourth grade; Fritz, from the eighth; and Craig, who you have known since tenth grade, but have been close friends since the first year of college.

Richard: We recently emailed, as Doug and his wife Nancy lived in Tennessee. One of the first things you asked Doug, who has consciously been assisting you, was when you would ask for his advice about this Journal project.

Amorella: When you began working on the first chapter, you asked Doug if he remembered being Juniors at Westerville High, a Friday Spring night with you in your 1949 Ford, as you were driving on a quiet two-lane county road east of the small town of Sunbury. Low dark clouds prevailed, and you were conversing about the reality of UFOs, one of your primary shared interests.

On other such occasions, you both had driven about on such lonely, mostly farm roads hoping you might see a UFO on a more transparent night. You came upon a crossroad with a small church on one corner. When you stopped at the sign, you both looked up and saw what appeared to be two small crosses of light on the dark clouds. It grew eerily quiet. You both looked to the roof and steeple of the wood-clad church for floodlights that might shine from the church top up to the low clouds, but you both witnessed no such light. After a few moments, you turned south, driving back towards Westerville. Is this not so?

Richard: Yes. He had not thought about the incident but did recollect it when I asked. We had never resolved what had happened, but you have since thought there could have been two flood lights hidden at two bottom corners of the steeple that might give such an appearance on low dark clouds. Looking back, most likely, this was the case, but it became an uncannily eerie night when we stopped and looked up, observing the white outline of two crosses on those threatening-weather clouds. We had long felt unconsciously connected, like intuitive soul brothers perhaps; that's why we were close friends and still are.

Amorella: What, then, are you suggesting, orndorff?

Richard: Doug's fundamental analysis of this project has brought us closer. As such, we are closest friends by the measure of time (friends since the third/fourth grade). We both feel drawn into this book project because of the curiously added spiritual interest. I appreciate the advice I received from my friends. Doug has corresponded with the most detail. He is showing the most inner connection to the project.

Amorella: There is an inner truth to your observations. I suspect this shared mutual observation is an innately shared spiritual and scientific interest. You are the oldest and, therefore, closest in shared friendship from one heartansoulanmind to the other. You are already sharing this experience, which is a positive direction. You need to show constant clarity, orndorff; that's fine in this type of project. Besides, you are supposed to be dead, remember?

Richard: You have a great sense of humor, Amorella. I am trying to understand what I'd do if you did not.

Amorella: *The morning has been relaxing since the day's chores are done. Jadah just left your lap for the green jungle detailed chair on your right as you face north on the windy, warm, and partly cloudy Saturday morning. The usual flock variety of birds is out, about, and on the tubular feeder. The lowland dip in the backyard still has seeable standing water until you walk almost to the west neighbor's property line. It is fifty-eight degrees presently and with a flag-stiffening breeze. Spring. Even some lower branches of the bushes have sprouted light patches of green. And observe the clouds clearing a bit, and blue is showing through.*

Richard: I enjoy reading your words, Amorella. I wish I could also describe it; I love the flow, cadence, and circumstance.

Amorella: *And, all before noon, young man.*

Amorella: *You are at Alum Creek Dam next to the college and facing north toward the row of pine. As it has just rained, few people are out, a couple of fishermen and a couple on a walk with the broken clouds and now blue skies between. You had a McD's fish sandwich, large Diet Coke, and a few more cookies than you should have since they gave you four because of the long wait.*

Richard: I knew better than to eat the extra two, but I did anyway because they were still warm. If someone gives me a warm chocolate chip cookie, it is almost impossible to turn it down. Once dead, all we'll have is the memory, hopefully. If not, what difference does it make?

26 March 2023, Sunday

Amorella: You relaxed with the cats, and at one-fifteen, you began relaxing with Carol until just after six o'clock this evening. You two took a Sunday drive over along Hoover Dam up to Galena, then down to north Westerville, again to Sunbury for McD's sundaes, and over to Africa Road to home. Once home, the cats were fed, and you rested on the bed for about forty-five minutes before moving to the Lanai for another forty-five. Then you took the car to Mellow Mushroom for their House Special, split a medium pizza with a Diet Coke each, and brought the other half home after dropping Carol off at The Gables at six-ten o'clock. Home with Jadah on your lap.

Amorella: You watched ABC News, then turned off the television shortly after. You finished reading the Sunday Dispatch, but while on the editorial page, you found an article on spiritualism, the good and bad points. The good point was that it had to begin with the Spirit of G-D, but you disagree. Spiritualism must begin with G-D is G-D. That's how your heartansoulanmind sees it.

Richard: Again, you surprise me, Amorella. You speak a truth I concur with only because you used "G-D is G-D" and not G-D. As such, you surprised me twice. 'G-D is G-D' is my base rather than G-D because it is more inclusive, not because it appears repetitive as a reinforcer. I had not considered this before reading the article titled, "The Danger of Unanchored Spirituality" by Shayne Looper, a guest columnist.

Amorella: You responded more quickly than you thought, which is also a surprise. Why did you respond so quickly to the article, orndorff?

Richard: I responded more quickly than I felt I was going to. Instead of jumping ahead, I returned to what is a 'sacred definition' (to me) of G-D: being 'G-D is G-D.' I always go to a definition, whether it is in the dictionary as such or not.

Amorella: Are you going to apologize for calling it a 'sacred definition'?

Richard: No.

Amorella: What if, hypothetically, G-D would ask you to apologize?

Richard: I would say, "No," then ask, "Why should I apologize for what my 'heart' says first, and from what my 'soulanmind' might shrink to in responding? Is that even an ethical thought, Amorella? Is it an ethical thought? I ask because it should appear as a virtuous thought, not a moral or philosophical one.

Hypothetically, how does one respond if G-D asks me a question which may be plausible with an active heartansoulanmind while physically dead? Such a scenario does not exist in philosophy or ethics, yet people talk and write about communicating directly with G-D. At least, this is how I understand it. There may be a rule on communicating with G-D if G-D hypothetically asks a heartansoulanmind a question.

I answered the question by responding with my heart as separate from soul and mind and explaining why. With me, there can be too much bickering between soul and mind. And, as stated in an earlier chapter, the spiritual heart is supposedly a gift from G-D. – But, of course, this work is a journal format.

The hypothetical is from the lesser natural gift. I am thinking along this pathway of logic and reason, which is my sense of ethics in this hypothetical circumstance. I see no reason to be humble when asking a heartfelt question. Pause. Suddenly, my humility prevails, and I shut up because I have nothing else to say.

Amorella: When you have something to say, you spout every word out and are done without being mannerly about it.

Richard: My spiritual heart does not know politeness; it gets to the point as best it can and then shuts up. I am not going to apologize for that.

Amorella: The Reader may see Mr. Orndorff is sometimes stubborn.

Richard: I don't care what you do with this, Amorella. Good night, my spiritual friend.

Amorella: Good night, Richard. Good night to you and the Readers, also.

27 March 2023, Monday

Amorella: You woke up at about four-ten for no reason other than to go to the bathroom, then realized I hadn't washed the clothes for a week or so. You also quickly noted that you had yet to take the bed sheets out of the dryer two weeks ago. However, they were in good shape because you had ensured they were dry. You are awake. So, here you are with Jadah climbing up for a snuggle.

Richard: I've been sleeping lightly, rambling through my mind. This is the story of my everyday secret life.

Amorella: Heartanmind, mindanheart, heartanmind on a spin wash.

Richard: That's a good analogy, Amorella. That is on point for a conscious and imaginary life. This began after being introduced to faeries in a children's book, contrary to the reality of understanding everyday living (ages three and four). Daily living includes having and growing a physical body and recognizing the time I felt Jesus was my friend from Sunday school (ages five to seven). I didn't have this specific thought before, at least presently, but who knows?

Amorella: Why does it matter whether you have had this thought before or not?

Richard: It matters because I would be repeating myself, especially now that I am supposed to be theoretically dead.

Amorella: So then, what do you plan on doing now that you are theoretically dead?

Richard: I don't know. I suppose that is what this "reflecting on what life was" is all about. What to do next?

Amorella: That is a reasonable assumption for someone who is still living.

Richard: That is an interestingly worded comment. I need to 'consciously shut down' and sleep the rest of the night.

Amorella: A question: what if I left you just like that; puff. I'm gone?

Richard: I would feel lonely spiritually, but I would continue writing this. It is interesting to me from a projective perspective, and, like I have said before, if there is no afterlife, then what's the harm? If there is an afterlife, it may not be what we are projecting. I don't have a problem with that. Either way, it gives me an added projection on my heartansoulanmind future. Life is interesting, even coming to its conclusion. If you are my imagination, Amorella, so be it. Besides, I enjoy writing, and you or my imagination is worth noting when I have nothing else. It gives me something to do in my head.

Amorella: That's not very sentimental, orndorff.

Richard: No, it is not. Life is not sentimental either, though some memories are. Memories are all one takes with herorhim when one dies if one takes anything. I feel we have heartsansoulsanminds and G-D is G-D. I'll let it go at that.

Richard: I made a mistake a short time ago when I wrote, "I would feel spiritually lonely, but I would probably continue writing this up to today. . .." That is not true. I would have to stop writing because this is a conversation. I cannot have a meaningful conversation with myself.

Amorella: That is not true, and you know it.

Richard: You are right. Shakespeare's *Hamlet* shows one can have a meaningful, even artful, conversation with herorhimself. I am not bright enough to play the fool. The above passage is an excellent example of why. I become waterlogged. That's how I feel my mind is saturated and bobbing in the undercurrents below a dam. My mind feels catatonic.

Amorella: This book is a part of your permanent record of yourself, of who you are, dead or not.

Richard: If this work is part of a permanent record of my life, it becomes nonfiction, not speculative.

Amorella: *The work is nonfiction. It is your thoughts. Readers might assume the part I play is a prop, a way to show your story.*

Richard: I don't feel you are a prop. Why should you feel like you are a prop? Pause. Never mind, I don't want to know. I'm tired, Amorella. I might nap like my furry little friend curled up in the jungle leaf print chair on my right is doing.

Richard: I watched *NBC News*. I needed to see how this day's writing ties into the book.

Amorella: *This is not a novel, boy. You are writing about your life, who you were, and who you are now dead. When people review their lives, they check their memories and how they remember them, but it is more than that. From a literary perspective, this day's work needs to make more sense because you are trained to critique stories for elements that make up a good story. However, this work is not literature in that sense; it is not a journal like A Journal of the Plague Year, published in 1722 by Daniel Defoe about the Great Plague of London in 1665. This literary work is about your life and what you must learn from it to better reflect your naked heartansoulanmind. Ironically, these words are the clothing you wear when you are dead, orndorff.*

Richard: Your words remind me of how vulnerable I feel I am.

30 March 2023, Thursday

Amorella: During September 1972, there was more readjusting to the classroom than you expected. These administrators had a far greater range of power and control than at Graded. Overall, you found the rules about teachers and students fair and just. Different directions, but rules nevertheless. Your authority in the classroom was by intent: "Be courteous and polite." Students tested you for a time or two, but you survived. The students and faculty also took a liking to you because: 1. you had taught overseas in Brazil at an educationally well-known American private school, Escola Graduada. One of the most important members of the department to you personally was Lyn Van Aiken.

31 March 2023, Friday

Richard: I was sitting in the living room chair thinking about Lyn Van Aiken and what to say about those years at Indian Hill. I am using my memories of Lyn to guide me through those years. There were two other teachers who guided me along the way before I left and began teaching at Wm. Mason High in the 1984-1985, they were Jim Powers and Bill Kincaid. Bill helped keep me hired at Mason just before I earned tenure at Mason in 1987 because one of Mason's school board members had been a student of his. He reassured her; and she explained to the others on the Board that I was a very good teacher worth keeping.

On February 22, 1991, my very good, and retired friend at Indian Hill, Lyn was killed in a Chilean airline LAN plane crash on a remote Chilean Navarino island when it overshot the runway. My other friend, Jim Powers, was along and survived. They were traveling on the Pacific side of South America from

Lima to Antarctica and then up the Atlantic side to Buenos Aries and Rio de Janeiro.

Amorella: We can move from this to your memory at Indian Hill.

Richard: In the first year at Indian Hill High School, I felt I floundered a bit, particularly in ninth-grade honors classes. I followed the curriculum to the letter and revised and updated the propaganda unit. I had novels to teach as well as grammar. We used *Warriner's English Grammar and Composition 9,* publishers, Harcourt, Brace & World, Inc., 1963 edition, and a Vocabulary Workbook. I don't remember the novels other than *A Separate Peace, Fahrenheit 451, Watership Down,* and sometimes *Lord of the Flies,* but they were appropriate, as were *The Scarlet Letter and To Kill A Mockingbird.*

I had read them and felt comfortable teaching from books. *Romeo and Juliet,* Shakespeare's standard, was introduced in most first-year public school classes, and almost everyone had seen the 1968 film. Life was so much easier if you had good interested students who saw the film first. It is difficult for many media-oriented students that age, and even through high school, to read a play first.

Amorella: What was your value as a teacher?

Richard: I am still determining what my value was. I don't think I ever thought about my value as a teacher. I focused on having students learn to think for themselves and how, when reading or listening, to separate the bullshit from the real thing.

Amorella: *Those lines just above could have been better expressed.*

Richard: No, they aren't well expressed, as you say; but the words aren't bullshit.

OPEN

Chapter Seventeen

2 April 2023, Sunday

Richard: I am at Alum Creek Park, down near the dam.

Amorella: In 1975, you and Carol built a modest bi-level house in Mason, Ohio. Carol was teaching fourth grade at Blue Ash and you were at Indian Hill.

Richard: Our new house, at the time, was in a development on the west side of Mason. The town was built along State Route 42. Mason was a small Ohio farm town known for two things, the powerful WLW transmission station, northeast of our backyard, about a mile away as the crow flies, and the nearby Bethany Relay Station, the first Voice of America station constructed in the United States in 1944. The Wikipedia descriptions of both are below.

WLW

"WLW's distinctive diamond-shaped antenna is featured on the official seal of the City of Mason. Designed and erected by Blaw-Knox Tower company in 1934, it was the second of its type to be built, after WSM's in Nashville, Tennessee, and is one of eight still operational in the United States.

WLW's 500,000-watt "RCA 1" transmitter was in operation between 1934 and 1939 and was the highest power ever used in the United States for public, domestic radio broadcasting. It was designed as an amplifier of the regular 50 kW transmitter. It operated in class C with high-level plate modulation, requiring two dedicated 33-kilovolt electrical substation lines and an oversized cooling pond with spray fountains. It ran with a power input of about 750 kW (plus another 400 kW of audio for the modulator) to produce 500 kW. Even after 1939, when regular WLW programming was prohibited from operating with more than 50,000 watts, the station continued post-midnight high-powered operation as experimental station W8XO, which helped to improve the RCA 1 transmitter's power and reliability. By the end of World War II, it could produce one million watts, and it "loafed along" at 600 kW."

Bethany Relay Station

"The Voice of America's Bethany Relay Station was located in Butler County, Ohio's Union Township, about 25 miles (40 km) north of Cincinnati, adjacent to the transmitter site of WLW. Starting in 1944 during World War II, it transmitted American radio programming abroad on shortwave frequencies, using 200,000-watt transmitters built by Crosley engineers under the direction of R.J. Rockwell. The site was developed to provide 'fallback' transmission facilities inland and away from the East Coast, where transmitters were located in Massachusetts, on Long Island in New York, and in New Jersey, all close to the ocean, subject to attack from German submarines or other invading forces. Programming originated from studios in New York until 1954, when VOA headquarters moved to Washington. The station operated until 1994. The facility took its name from the Liberty Township community of Bethany, about two miles north of the facility.

In 1943, the United States government bought nearly all of Section 12 of Township 3, Range 2 of the Symmes Purchase, the northeastern-most section of Union Township. . ... The site was chosen for its elevation and its shallow bedrock and is today bounded by Tylersville Road on the south, Cox Road to the west, Liberty Way to the north, and Butler-Warren Road.

The transmitters were built by Powel Crosley Jr.'s Crosley Broadcasting Corporation about one mile west of the company's tower for WLW-AM in Mason. The Office of War Information began broadcasting in July 1944, and Adolf Hitler is said to have denounced the "Cincinnati liars." Following the war, with the OWI abolished, the facility was taken over by the State Department in 1945. It became part of the newly created United States Information Agency in 1953. The Crosley Broadcasting Corporation operated the facility for the government until November 1963, when the Voice of America assumed direct control.

At its peak, the facility had six transmitters broadcasting with 250 kW and two transmitting with 50 kW.

The facility was closed on 14 November 1994; the transmissions shifted to satellites because of changing technologies. As a result, the towers were brought down from December 1997 to February 1998."

Amorella: Both stations were within a mile of the Orndorff home and became a focal point in Richard's heartansoulanmind.

Richard: I didn't realize this, Amorella. Thinking back, though, I did become preoccupied with their history of social influence. It was interesting, particularly the ground waves from the VOA. They were known to affect nearby cars, farmers could hear the stations on wooden fence posts, which acted as speakers occasionally, and we could pick up VOA through the wood beams in the ceiling and walls. It was spooky. Once in a while, the wood beams would pick up WLW, also. How could I have forgotten about that? It was both interesting science-wise and spooky-wise. It might have attracted UFOs. I'll checked it out.

5 Famous & Elusive Ohio UFO Cases

"Buckeye State ranks 8ᵗʰ for most sighting in the U.S."

By Matt Bayman

According to research conducted by Outforia and based on reports filed with the National UFO Reporting Center, Ohio ranks 8ᵗʰ overall in the United States for the most UFO sightings. Since the 1950s, more than 4,100 reports have been filed in the Buckeye State, including many in western Ohio.

Most sightings had simple explanations, such as weather balloons, military aircraft, or some kind of weather or astronomical phenomena. However, quite a few remain unexplained.

With this in mind, here are five of Ohio's most compelling and notorious unsolved UFO cases, including some that occurred in our backyard and several of which involved Wright-Patterson Air Force Base and its famous UFO investigative unit, Project BLUE BOOK.

1973: The Great UFO Wave of 1973 – Preventing Nuclear War?

Something was going on in the skies above Ohio in October of 1973, but whether or not it was an alien invasion of some kind or just the U.S. Armed Forces responding to a potential nuclear threat in the Middle East is up for debate. Some believe, however, that it was both.

Cincinnati, Ohio, 17 October

The [Hamilton] County Sheriff's Office receives between 30 and 40 reports of "shiny objects zigzagging through the sky." A police sergeant near Cincinnati reports chasing a white and yellow craft, later saying, "I never believed in UFOs until tonight."

A family in Hamilton also sees an object half the size of a football field flying over their home without making any noise.

So far, with one or two exceptions, these reports can be explained based on what the military was up to.

Along with pulling off Operation NICKEL GRASS, the military may have been running large-scale training exercises to prepare for war, which could have involved stealth helicopters and other secret aircraft in the rural countryside.

If anyone has ever seen the massive C-5 airplanes at Wright-Patterson conducting quick-landing drills (often using State Route 202 as a measuring guide), it is an otherworldly experience. The planes are enormous but almost appear stationary on the horizon, making extremely low ground sweeps. It looks completely unreal. Every time the base runs these exercises, they must notify the local media so people don't become alarmed.

Richard: The above is a sample. I included it because it does suggest Wright-Patterson Air Force Base could be a partial reason for the "lights in the sky" – probably ninety-nine percent of them, in my opinion.

Amorella: Why this reaction to these UFO sightings, Richard?

Richard: I think most of the UFO material might as well be hogwash. It has taken on a life of its own as far as the media is concerned. I don't know why you want to include it.

Amorella: Do you think the UFO inclusion violates your attempt to keep the Journal focused on something more down to earth, like spiritual issues instead?

Richard: You really know how to ask the right question, Amorella. I give you credit. I have no more comments at this time. This question really pisses me off.

Amorella: Does it now. Why is that?

Richard: I don't know. It is keeping me honest. You are right, once again. Why am I getting so angry?

Amorella: You are still peeved.

Richard: I am. I don't know why. UFOs, that's what we are talking about.

Amorella: Do you see why this material needs to be added? It is about what you still are: angry.

Richard: The anger?

Amorella: The same anger you have always had.

Richard: I suppose it goes back to happenings in Chapter One.

Amorella: Possibly, but doubtful.

Richard: The only thing I can come up with is Indian Hill had gotten a new superintendent my third or fourth year. The school board hired someone with a strong objective/goals orientation for teachers, and by 1978 I was not too happy about it. I had acquired my basic classroom procedures, goals, and objectives by then. Mine were humanitarian-oriented; the Board of Education's goals and objectives were business and humanitarian-oriented. These two orientations started a professional struggle brewing within me. Being my usual lazy self, I reformed my humanitarian purposes into business goals and objectives as best I could – this was out-and-out manipulation, and I knew it from the get-go. I was being honest with myself and dishonest with the Board.

Amorella: There you are. This brought about another district of discontent in the school year 1977-1978. You began writing dark-humored poetry once again and something new, a first novel.

199

Richard Henry Orndorff

Richard: The unpublished novel was a James Bond-type thriller, <u>No Time To Die</u> was the working title, and it took place partially in Brazil, Bolivia, and Peru. It was a fun escape from the situation at school. One of the main things I kept and adapted to my later books was the plane, a 1978 Cessna Centurion turboprop with an air-pressured cabin. It had a single prop and held six passengers and luggage.

I did my research, and the only item I had utterly wrong originally was where the fuel cap was. An education resource professional at school told me her husband worked at the control tower at the Cincinnati airport across the river in Northern Kentucky. He had been used as an aircraft specialist in several significant crashes in the United States. She asked him independently, and he volunteered to talk with me. I was so pumped; a real specialist would look over the draft.

He read the selections concerning the plane. He showed me changes to make from the pilot's perspective (such as facts I could not have considered with a craft that size flying through the Andes Mountains), and he noted where the fuel intake was. From what I could tell, I had the wrong location, searching for information long before the Internet. I wanted a plausible story in that if a pilot read the novel, sheorhe would at least realize I had done the research. All those Microsoft Game flights were the only thing I had going for me. I got the old game out and began playing it again, using a plane close to the Cessna Centurion. Wow, Amorella. Fun. I forgot all this.

Amorella: *Take a break.*

Amorella: You are atop the hill overlooking the Alum Creek Reservoir dam off Lewis Center Road. You had Friday's McD's cold apple oatmeal for lunch, a Zero candy bar, and a diet cherry Coke from home. Kim sent a text, and you are going to their house for supper tonight at about four-thirty. Dinner is at five-thirty. You are obviously still excited about the Cessna.

Richard: I am. I wish I could remember the names of those people, especially the aircraft specialist and his wife. I could have them in old notes. I always kept notes.

Amorella: You can work on that later if you have the time and inclination. I understand your saying; anger is from the heart, not the mind. So, another district of heartanmind activity was the novel and dark-humored poetry, some of which you had published in small independent poetry magazines in Ohio and California.

Richard: How do you remember California? There was a green soft-covered National Poetry magazine published there. How do you remember that?

Amorella: You had it in the basement while searching for the Indian Hill yearbook.

Richard: Yes, that is true. I can see it in my head as I put it aside. – Is that me remembering originally here, or was it you? But then, I suddenly remembered seeing myself place the magazine aside on top of another on a box to my right.

Amorella: That is the trick, isn't it, orndorff. Who, of the two of us, remembers what-first, in selected incidences used?

201

Richard: Is this a weakness in our link? How would I discover this?

Amorella: In your auditory imagination, you are, in imagination, tuning into the voice of HAL in 2001 Space Odyssey. You are automatically picking up my written voice and transposing, listening to it as you silently read my words.

Richard: Yes, you are correct, but when I read your name, it was in my usual auditory voice for you, not HAL's. Now, that is interesting. Why would I have developed such a discriminating aural imagination for you in the first place?

Amorella: Perhaps from when you spoke to and listened to the faeries when you were four and five.

Richard: Unbelievable. Is this possible? It's no wonder I privately don't know who I am sometimes. In my head, I am who I think or imagine myself to be. If so, it is no wonder I have led such a private and somewhat confusing personal life. How very unconventional. What an odd thing to have happened. This was never considered in sessions with two psychologists in the 1980s. In any case, I learned to adapt to it and not feel it real in my world with other people. If the slightest of hypotheses are working here, I may have faked it. Nobody knows, including myself . . . unbelievable.

Amorella: Time for a break, orndorff. Pause. Too lonely up on top, you are now down by the Westerville dam at your usual handicapped parking spot under naked trees, watching fishermen laboring to catch something under the glare of a semi-bright sun between the haze and clouds. Why don't we use the time to put all this in a separate document, labeling it Chapter Seventeen?

Richard: That's fine with me, Amorella.

Amorella: Let's call it a chapter.

OPEN

Chapter Eighteen

5 April 2023, Wednesday

Amorella: In the 1990s, Mason became a separate city school system in Warren County and a much larger school. Below is from Wikipedia

Mason City Schools (officially the Mason City School District) is a city school district primarily serving Mason and Deerfield Township in Warren County, Ohio, United States. As of 2018, the community has 10,627 students. Its high school, William Mason High School, is the largest in Ohio by enrollment.

History

Mason's first school was on Main Street and stood until the 1960s. New buildings were built for Mason High School on North East Street in 1911, 1936, and 1953. All three are now district administrative offices. Mason Heights Elementary School opened in 1967.

In the 1990s and 2000s, Mason City Schools grew significantly as Cincinnati's urban sprawl pushed northward into Warren County, and Mason became Ohio's fastest-growing city. Procter & Gamble opened a Health Care Research Center that spurred construction on almost 40 new subdivisions in Mason. From 1990 to 2002, the district tripled enrollment from 2,653 students in four buildings to 8,100 students in seven. By 1998, it had become Mason's fifth-largest employer, with a $23 million annual budget and 574 employees. The district responded to funding and overcrowding concerns by opening a new middle school in 1994, signing a 10-year, $1.1 million contract with Pepsi in 1997, and opening the $71.9 million, three-story, 379,000-square-foot (35,200 m2) William Mason High School in September [2002]. District enrollment doubled between 1999 and 2009 before peaking at 11,000 around 2013. A $30 million addition to the high school opened in 2009.

Wikipedia

Richard: That's very different from when I joined Mason Local Schools. My closest personal friend all those years was Gary Poppelwell, a guidance counselor and neighbor. That was Mason; and when I retired at the end of the 2002-2003 school year. They were still working on parts of the school that year. We were living in the Lakeside subdivision across the street from the school in 1992. What a time it was.

Amorella: Kimberly Jean Orndorff's senior year begins at the brick-built Mason High School on Rt. 42. It had been renovated and enlarged during her last four years as a student.

Richard: I had Kim for Advanced Placement English Literature her senior year. She had earned an A average in her junior English class and planned on taking AP. This was a unique family experience. I really had no doubts. We got along well and continued to do so throughout the year and still do.

Amorella: Few parents have their children in classes because some feel it would appear unfair to the other students, and unjustly so for the teacher's son or daughter. There was no doubt in anyone's mind that Kim was his favorite daughter. They may have expected Mr. Orndorff would select her to be his number one student. Not the case. Kim earned an A-. That's what she worked for, an A-.

Richard: Kim's junior year of French continued with French teacher, Mrs. Gwen Goode, teaching her child, Robert, French because no one else taught the course. There had been no problems. There were no problems in my class either, probably because the two had been in the same classes since the school system was much smaller in the early days. I had Robert in my senior college prep class because he did not elect to take AP. There were no problems.

Kim graduated, as did the rest of her Mason High School in 1997. She was looking forward to beginning classes at Miami University, Oxford, Ohio, in the coming Fall. Carol and I were pleased and proud at our scholarly daughter's graduation.

6 April 2023, Thursday

Amorella: Carol and Richard's next three years passed quickly. Richard self-published his first science fiction novel of 69,660 words, Stuck, under the pen name O. H. Richards. It was published by a relatively new self-publishing press, iUniverse, in 2001. This is from the edited overview on the blue back cover.

"Stuck" is a lightly satirical and philosophical fiction presented through the observations of Friendly, a human-like marsupial with a pouch, and her subconscious writing assistant, Soki, in 1988. Friendly (and one of her ship mates, Fargo) arrives on Earth to find only four adult human beings alive. The two marsupials use scientific means to ensure the human species does not die out. One of their primary reasons for visiting Earth in the first place is because humans (like themselves) have a developed sense of spiritual consciousness.

Upon returning to Earth twelve years later, Friendly discovers the planet is as we knew it in 2000. Billions of people are alive, unaware they should have died from an unknown disease or biological mishap.

What does a good marsupial do under the circumstances? While waiting for her comrades to arrive. Friendly focuses on the human neighbors in a wealthy suburb of Chicago near where she positions her hidden spacecraft. She follows Justin, an American archeologist, his spouse, Pyl, a college art professor, and her brother, Blake, an independent scientist. Each has an agenda that does not include an alien marsupial named Friendly."

The author, Richard, turned three the day Hiroshima was bombed. He began cartooning science fiction to get off this planet when he was six. The writer is what he is, a crusty gray-bearded misanthrope who loves his wife, daughter, family, students, Plato, Aristotle, Chaucer, Shakespeare, Milton, Melville, and pizza.

Back Cover of *Stuck*

Amorella: Richard finished the second novel, <u>Home</u>, and was working on a third titled, On Earth, during his last years of teaching. <u>Stuck</u>, <u>Home</u>, and <u>On Earth</u> was supposedly a trilogy, but never published the other two.

Richard retired from teaching at the end of the school year 2002-2003. Carol retired from teaching at the end of the next year, 2003-2004.

Amorella: *When you were conversing with Fritz at lunch during those times, you once said that your words for the books come from directly from your unconsciousness; that you never know what Amorella will write.*

Richard: So, you are suggesting that my unconsciousness has a partial spiritual form. I somehow got the idea that I might have a tiny alien in my head, like the little alien character in the books.

Amorella: *This is what you do. You compartmentalize. Your consciousness is a district in your head that you have accepted as having a possible tiny alien within because you have confusion and difficulties in understanding your humanity as a totality. You are parts, not a whole. You feel and have felt something is missing within your mind, if not your heartansoul. This is not the case. You feel you are a human sum of pieces, but you, indeed, are a whole person.*

Richard: If this is so, where does G-D fit into this humanity of parts or wholeness?

Amorella: *You were interrupted by Jadah, who needed warmth, held, and a little attention for a few minutes. What were you thinking about while holding her? This is what:*

209

"Why did I use 'lip of her pouch' with Friendly in the bath? Why didn't I use the 'cusp of her pouch'? It would probably have been more accurate."

Amorella: What's with the accuracy, orndorff. Friendly is a marsupial character in your story. You say you are parts, not a whole. Yet, you picture Friendly, a character, a reality, a physical being.

Richard: She's like the Faeries when I was a kid. That's pretty good, Amorella. I like it.

Amorella: The truth is that the adult alien Friendly is in many ways the young Faery in your youth. That's my point.

Richard: I don't consciously agree. I don't want this book to be about me, Amorella. Yet, it appears to be heading that way. Rather, I want this book to be about being a human being.

Amorella: We are writing this book essentially so when you are dead, you will find it easier knowing who you are and accepting it wholeheartedly.

Richard: Well, then we want two different things. I can separate my imagination for writing from reality, but not when I am writing. If I did, it would be discovered by a Reader. My honesty would appear a dishonest reinterpretation, I would be, to myself, a fake writer. A real writer has to focus on the truth of what a human being is, not what is wishful in being human. I attempt to remain as much as possible, detached and objective thinking in life.

Richard: I like to see my concept of G-D, written as a fact, but in reality, what is between the lines is white paper or an electric-like simulation of white paper. So, between the lines, I view G-D as an inference – so much for being detached and objective.

Amorella: Richard, are you trying to defend G-D as a Spirit Being?

Richard: G-D exists. I use reason, logic, and emotional appeal. G-D is G-D.

Amorella: You think there might be a way to prove G-D exists, but you need to know what it is.

Richard: How do you read my mind? Is privacy not sacred? How did we get to this point anyway? I wasn't thinking about G-D. I was thinking about the human heartansoulanmind, the heartansoulanmind every human being has, indeed not my own heartansoulanmind. I don't even want to exist. Deep down, I don't think I ever did want to exist. There, that's my heartansoulanmind talking. What do you think? Never mind, I don't want to know, Amorella.

I love life. I love consciousness and thought, being a physical creature with a heartansoulanmind. Being here, alive, is different than I imagined it would be. This concept of not existing is nothing more than another disheartened district in my mind. I'm done. I have nothing else to write today.

211

OPEN

Chapter Nineteen

*I am **Humanella**. You met me earlier in another chapter. I was once a human spirit, who joined with another human spirit some few centuries ago. A human spirit is not of The Amorella. The Amorella are Spirits who help the once living adjust to a spiritual existence. Some recently physically dead find Humanella easier to adjust with because we were once living, just as you, the Reader, are. We assist The Amorella when needed. I find it quite satisfying to help others of my living, half-spiritual, species. The spiritual half of a person is not living and never was. This might help construct a different viewpoint. There is no timeline. This helps adjusting also.*

It is as though the tables are turned, so to speak. Now, you might better adjust to being a spirit; just as your spirit has been trying to adjust to being half a physical living human being during your lifetime. This is an analogy. Mathematics as human understand it, does not exist. Physics does not exist either. Words alone exist. When expressed thoughtfully and directly, that is, consciously they are then understood by others. Communication exists. Memories exist. The heartansoulanmind of a once living human being exists. Communication is for cooperation, understanding, and self-expression of the heartansoulanmind. It is Understood through thought alone, without language. In a sense the spirit language is as the facial expressions one showed in life. The spirit is only a two-dimensional face, but when communicating directly with another heartansoulanmind, it appears, ever so slightly, to be three dimensional. This brings the greatest of joy to human spirits. The chapter continues.

7 April 2023, Friday

Richard: Secretly, I am an idealist. I despise this because idealism can lead to corruption – the idealism of Communism, for instance, and perhaps even the idealism of democracy. I note these separate districts in my mind that are who I am, but I adjusted to let them co-exist over the years.

Humanella: You have adjusted because you must do so to survive as an individual. You feel you had no choice, consciously or unconsciously, orndorff.

Richard: I agree, Humanella, on principle. I am learning things about myself I did not consciously realize. The districts-in-the-mind concept are good because though the districts are seemingly scattered everywhere in my mind, they are all connected to who I am as a human being. This is my observation. I separate that part unconsciously and then consciously ignore its existence.

Humanella: You separate one part of yourself unconsciously, then consciously ignore its existence. If this is true, you need to better control your unconscious tendencies.

Richard: One cannot completely control the unconscious.

Humanella: But you do, to an extent, by separating yourself into districts. That is how you learn to survive consciously and unconsciously.

Richard: It is a weird and awkward way to do something.

Humanella: *It seems inefficient to you?*

Richard: Yes, it does. Very odd, this is. Irregular, in fact, in keeping a clear mind from clutter and a cluttered mind from being clear and regular. If I do this, it is a human thing to do, and somehow, other humans may also do this: separate the unlikable unconsciously, then consciously ignore its existence.

Humanella: *There you are, orndorff. You thought it through. Time for a break; either get up and read the paper or sleep.*

Richard: That is a rather strange comment, Humanella.

Humanella: *You went to sleep. Now you are up and have fed the cats and cleaned their litter box. The clouds are still here even though it was an incredible sunset. Everything is regular like you prefer, old man. Have a good day.*

Richard: I was about to respond out of habit: "You have a good day, too." I have a question. How is the environment in my head, Amorella? Since you don't have days and nights?

Humanella: *I'm not in your head, orndorff. Not everything is about you.*

Richard: I agree. This is about who I consciously think I am now that I am feigning death. It is not the same thing.

Humanella: *I didn't expect that. How are they different?*

Richard: This book business, the set-up, is detached from me, the person typing. I am the person behind the fingertips. I could not do this if this were not from my perspective. When at the computer, my fingertips are a loan-free gift for Amorella. I like her, and in this setting, I am think of you as a friend, maybe like the Faeries of my younger days.

I let Amorella write. I lend her my fingertips because she is real to me; that is, I do not view you as my imagination, not a hallucination. Your words are not my words. I am the old fellow with the imagination I have always had, the imagination my mother told me I had to put away. I know who I was, and what I am now: the same person, no different, and with similar experiences to other human beings. I am also the fellow at the other end of my fingertips that I loan out. I do this attempting to think objectively, to allow her your space, to possibly better see the world as it is, not how people think it is.

Humanella: How do you think people think the world is?

Richard: Most people, not all, think the world is about how they fit into the world privately and publicly. That way, their hearts and minds can function normally. And I am no different than anyone else on that score; however, my mindset is that the reality of experiencing life can be more objective by mentally detach from myself. If one can't see the world disconnected from her or himself, one can't see it objectively. One has to mentally reinvent the *self* to take this point of view. Self-hypnosis helps that happen for me.

When I figuratively stand beside my physical self, I mentally understand life better. I experience the world in some ways like I do not fully exist here; I find understanding the universe is a more realistic approach if I am not in it. The world obviously goes on whether we exist as individuals or not. These detached thinking purposes are not while having conversation with others, driving a car, watching your grandchildren or kissing your friend or wife or husband.

Humanella: *Do you feel this is how I, the Humanella, experience physical, material living. In a detachment?*

Richard: No, Humanella. I suppose you are a spiritual being as I accept Amorella. You would not be here if Amorella didn't allow it. You are not a legal resident on this planet presently. However, the reality is being conscious after physical death is a hypothetical.

It is my philosophical opinion that it is possible to be conscious yet physically declared dead. The evidence, to me, is that I have *your* thoughts through my typing. I understand your thoughts, like Amorella's, are not my conscious thoughts in this setting. I do not know your thoughts are not literally my unconscious thoughts. You, Humanella, may be just another part of myself, splintered off, so to speak. I can accept this because of my ability to detach, to view myself more objectively through self-hypnosis.

Humanella: *Take a break, orndorff. Have breakfast, get dressed, and feed the birds.*

Richard: Gladly, Humanella, I was not conscious of the time.

Richard: While searching through my boxes of notes and writings, I found the list of books that had made the most impressions on my thinking. In the late 1990s, at Miami

University, Oxford, Ohio, I was a student in a course to help learn how to better serve the needs of my students in their writing. The class of teachers from surrounding school districts were assigned to each write a list of the most influential authors and their books in our lives.

My list of authors and examples of their writings visited my college prep, honors, and advanced placement classrooms many times throughout my thirty-seven professional teaching years. This list acknowledges these authors who, from time to time, still visit my heartanmind. In this class work I put them in a haphazard order, because if I were going to consciously list them from first to last, it could take a lifetime of study, at least my allotted lifetime. This list is not imagined as a pile of books in the corner of a study or attic or basement. The essence of each rest in my heartansoulanmind and how in the world would I get the collection in a physical order if I had them altogether? I cannot imagine the energy it would take to decide each, put it on a shelf from best to last according to heart and mind. Which would be more important if it were a task after physical death? I'm leaving the soul out of this decision-making because as everyone knows the heart always wins out in choices of this sort.

If one is not a book reader, then films will do. One hundred of your favorite films or songs in order of heart and mind. My sense was that I had to decide through a silent discussion between heart and mind, and each response to the book would have to be weighed and considered and then, let's say, weighed by the soul who would then consult and discuss with the two parties what the soul recommended as book one through a hundred.

First, I developed my own personal speed-reading techniques in my twenties. How many was the goal, but it depended on the number of words and whether the book was fiction or nonfiction. In both case I had to absorb the reasoning as well as the character develop and theme. It also depended on how many essays of one type or another I had to read and grade with a separate content and grammar score. Classwork came first, almost always. This was my joyful private life. Truly. Mostly, I averaged two books a week. Sometimes three.

The most important people to me during those weeks were Carol, then Kim and Carol, I did not watch much television. – Sorry, I got carried away.

Humanella: *Drop in the list, Mr. Orndorff. I like that it was an assignment.*

Richard: What were your assignments?

Humanella: *I was a Greek soldier, a commander, whose interest was philosophy – in the three hundreds before your Jesus.*

Richard: Oh.

Humanella: *This is about you, and you are not even recently dead.*

Richard: This book is hypothetical.

Amorella *interrupts: This is project is set from my perspective. This work exist in orndorff's heartansoulanmind. On with the list:*

Richard: These titles are most important works I have read in my life to date: the late 1990s. These books molded aspects my character, my persona. Many of these showed me deeper, profound thought between the lines, and they helped me developed my personal sense of ethics. Many of the works altered my personal perspective on what life is and/or what living a good life should be about. – rho

The Oresteia – Aeschylus

The Word – I. Wallace

The Loved One – E. Waugh

Our Town – T. Wilder

Brave New World – A. Huxley

Totem and Taboo & Interpretation of Dreams – S. Freud

Paradise Lost – J. Milton

The Gallic Wars – J. Caesar

The Hero with a Thousand Faces – J. Campbell

Existentialism from Dostoevsky to Sartre – (ed.) W. Kaufman

History of the English-Speaking Peoples – W. Churchill

Henry V, Hamlet, Taming of the Shrew, Macbeth – Shakespeare

The New Golden Bough – J. Fraser

The Rockefellers – Collier & Horowitz

Extraordinary Endings – Panati

Childhood's End – A. C. Clarke

Metaphysics – W. H. Walsh

The Sacred and the Profane – M. Eliade

William Blake – K. Raine

Oedipus & Antigone – Sophocles

Foundation Trilogy – I. Asimov

Coney Island of the Mind – L. Ferlinghetti

House on the Strand – D. DuMaurier

Class – P. Fussell

1984 & Animal Farm – G. Orwell

Here I Stand – R. H. Bainton

The History of Knowledge – C. Van Doren

The Discoverers – D. J. Boorstin

Treasure Island – R. L. Stevenson

The Varieties of Religious Experience – W. James

The Man Who Mistook His Wife for a Hat – O. Sacks

Death of a Salesman – A. Miller

The Dune Trilogy – F. Herbert

Stranger in a Strange Land – R. Heinlein

Thus Spoke Zarathustra & Beyond Good and Evil – F. Nietzche;

The Republic – Plato

Ethics – Aristotle

Confessions – St. Augustine

The Canterbury Tales – G. Chaucer

Faust – J. Goethe

St. Joan – G. B. Shaw

Tom Jones – H. Fielding

Lady Chatterley's Lover – D. H. Lawrence

Ulysses – J. Joyce

Candide – Voltaire

The Crash of 79 – P. Erdman

The Sovereign State of ITT – A. Sampson

Moby Dick – H. Melville

The Prince – Machiavelli

Selected Essays – Montaigne

Civil Disobedience – H. D. Thoreau

Essays – R. W. Emerson

The Universe and Dr. Einstein – L. Barnett

The Angels and Us & Ten Philosophical Mistakes – M. J. Adler

The Iliad & The Odyssey – Homer

Mythology – E. Hamilton

The Greek Philosophers – R. Warner

The Exorcist – P. Beatty

The Bible

The Koran

The Rise and Fall of Adolph Hitler – W. L. Shirer;

Death of a President & Arms of Krupp – W. Manchester;

The Ancient Book of the Dead – (tr.) R. Faulkner/(ed.) C. Anderson;

Ringworld – L. Niven

The Left Hand of Darkness – U. Leguin

Native Son – R. Wright

The Time Machine – H. G. Wells

Codebreakers – D. Kahn

A Man Called Intrepid – W. Stevenson

Beyond Freedom and Dignity – B. F. Skinner

Man and His Symbols – C. Jung

Rime of the Ancient Mariner – S. T. Coleridge

Chaos – J. Gleick

The Andromeda Strain – M. Crichton

The Ascent of Man – J. Bronowski

The Jungle – U. Sinclair

Edgar Cayce: The Sleeping Prophet – J. Stern

Frankenstein – M. W. Shelley

This Perfect Day & *The Boys from Brazil* – I. Levin

On the Road – J. Kerouac

Howl – A. Ginsberg

Druids – M. Llywelyn

Burr – G. Vidal

The Crystal Cave – M. Stewart

Canticle for Leibowitz – W. M. Miller, Jr.

Thirteen Days – R. Kennedy

A Separate Peace – J. Knowles

The Grapes of Wrath – J. Steinbeck

On the Beach – N. Shute

Earth Abides – G. R. Stewart

The Peloponnesian Wars – Thucydides

Logic for Undergraduates – R. J. Kreyche

Plato for the Modern Age – R. S. Brumbaugh

The Straight Dope – C. Adams

One Day in the Life of Ivan Denisovich – A. Solzhenitsyn

Being and Nothingness & No Exit – J. P. Sartre

Upanishads (Confidential Teachings) – Indian Philosophy/ Religion

The Potting Shed – G. Greene

The World is my Home – J. A. Michener

Future Shock – A. Toffler

Lysistrata – Aristophanes

The Hairy Ape – E. O'Neill

The Cherry Orchard – A. Chekhov.

Humanella: A well-expressed original introduction of well-read literature, orndorff. There is still a truth to your occasional renewed memories of these authors and their works in one way or another. Sometimes, directly or between the lines, in our discussions.

Richard: Thank you kindly, Amorella. I'm glad I came upon this list. In the present quick rereading, I felt an individual joyousness I felt when I read the individual works earlier for the first time. Some I have reread. I am in awe of those books and the authors who wrote them. - heartansoulanmind. rho

Humanella: This brings sudden tears to your eyes, old man. A confirmation from heartansoulanmind.

Richard: I feel timid and embarrassed. Please, enough for now, Humanella.

Humanella: This is as good a time as any, Richard; let's make it a chapter.

Richard: Thank you, Humanella. . I can't believe how overwhelming this list of books, plays and authors are in my heart. This is such an embarrassing, extremely private secret to share. Such hot tears suddenly fall over nothing but strings of words, sentences, and paragraphs. I must be in madness.

Humanella: It is with passion and humility you read the authors' names and titles, orndorff, not madness.

OPEN

Chapter Twenty

12 April 2023, Wednesday

Humanella: You are wondering what's on the agenda today. It is funny that you accept me as an independent spirit reality with whom you would like to continue the dialogue as if chatting in a room.

Richard: I sense you as fellow human, Humanella. And, I can see us becoming close friends. You have a spiritual sense of place and have a memory of once living.

Humanella: The answer is in placement. In other words: literally, 'heartansoulanmind' is not the same when placed in the spirit world. The balance is off. The soul holds the other two in harmony, like the heart is on one end of the teeter-totter, and the mind is on the other. A sense of balance exists between the heart and mind with the soul in the middle.

First, I will define "striking out," not erasing, so you can better ascertain my reasoning for moving from a real-world 'balance' to a spirit-world Balance.' The capital B is for clarification purposes, not to show the balance is less than the Balance. One is in the physical world, the other in the Spirit World.

Richard: This is quite interesting. I love words and meanings. Amorella. I need to look up the balance.

Richard Henry Orndorff

1. Balance

noun

1 an even distribution of weight enabling someone or something to remain upright and steady: she lost her balance before falling | slipping in the mud but keeping their balance. • Sailing the ability of a boat to stay on course without adjustment of the rudder.

2 a condition in which different elements are equal or in the correct proportions: [in singular: try to balance work and relaxation | overseas investments can add balance to an investment portfolio. • stability of one's mind or feelings: the way to peace and personal balance. • [in singular] the relative volume of various sound sources: the balance of the voices is good. • Art harmony of design and proportion.

3 an apparatus for weighing, especially one with a central pivot, beam, and a pair of scales. • (the Balance) the zodiac sign or constellation Libra.

4 a counteracting weight or force. • (balance wheel) the regulating device in a mechanical clock or watch.

5 a predominating weight or amount; the majority: the balance of opinion was that work was more important than leisure.

6 a figure representing the difference between credits and debits in an account; the amount of money held in an account: he accumulated a healthy balance with the savings bank. • the difference between an amount due and paid: unpaid credit-card balances. • [in singular] an amount left over.

verb [with object]

1 keep or put (something) in a steady position so that it does not fall: a mug that she balanced on her knee. • [no object] Remain in a steady position without falling: Richard balanced on the ball of one foot.

2 offset or compare the value of (one thing) with another: the cost of obtaining such information needs to be balanced against its benefits. • counteract, equal, or neutralize the weight or importance of a person balancing his radical remarks with more familiar declarations. • establish equal or appropriate proportions of elements when they struggle to balance work and family life.

3 compare debits and credits in (an account), typically to ensure they are equal: the law requires the council to balance its books each year. • [no object] (of an account) have credits and debits equal: a surplus on the capital account to make the account balance.

PHRASES balance of payments the difference in total value between payments into and out of a country over a period: [as modifier]: a balance-of-payments deficit. balance of power

1 a situation in which nations of the world have roughly equal power.

2 the power a small group holds when larger groups are of equal strength. balance of trade; the difference in value between a country's imports and exports: a country with a worsening balance of trade in manufactured products. In the balance uncertain, at a critical stage: the person's survival hung in the balance for days. On balance, with all things considered: but on balance, he was pleased. Strike a balance choose a moderate course or compromise: she's decided to strike a balance between fashionable and accessible. tip the balance (of a circumstance or event) be the deciding factor; make the critical difference: in this tight race, a single group of voters could tip the balance three factors eventually tipped the balance in favor of comparatively lenient policies.

New Oxford American Dictionary

Balance - as used about the Spirit World. - Amorella.

noun

1 a condition where elements are equal or in the correct proportions.

2 a stability of one's mind and feelings.

Verb [with object] **1** Keep or put (something) in a steady position.

New Oxford American Dictionary

Richard: I like this very much, Humanella. It is crucial to have definitions. This is a matter of reaching a series of understandings.

Amorella: Yes, There is a spiritual sense in nouns and verbs. Refrain from concerning yourselves too much with the other parts of speech. It is easy to ascertain which noun or verb will work together.

Richard: Do you mean to infer that the spiritual nature of words has a sense of being, as in existing?

Humanella: In the sense that a word or words exist in the Spirit World; words take on the nature of being 'charged with spiritual energy.'

Richard: I am looking for another definition, energy.

Humanella: You have no choice, orndorff.

2. Energy

energy - noun (plural energies)

1 the strength and vitality required for sustained physical or mental activity: changes in the levels of vitamins can affect energy and well-being. • (energies) are a person's physical and mental powers, typically as applied to a particular task or activity: an alternative is to devote your energies to voluntary work.

2 Nuclear energy is derived from using physical or chemical resources, primarily to provide light and heat or to work machines.

3 Physics is the property of matter and radiation manifest as a capacity to perform work (such as causing motion or the interaction of molecules): a collision in which no energy is transferred. • a degree or level of energy possessed by something or required by a process: gamma rays at different energies.

ORIGIN mid 16ᵗʰ century (denoting force or vigor of expression): from French énergie, or via late Latin from Greek energeia, from en- 'in, within' + ergon 'work.

New Oxford American Dictionary

energy - noun - as used about the Spirit World. - Humanella

1. (energies) a heartansoulanmind can be applied to a particular task.

2. level of energy required by a spiritual process.

New Oxford American Dictionary

3. passion | noun

1 strong and barely controllable emotion: a man of impetuous passion. • a state or outburst of strong emotion: oratory in which he gradually turns himself into a passion. • intense sexual love: their all-consuming passion for each other | She nurses a passion for Thomas. • an intense desire or enthusiasm for something: the English have a passion for gardens. • a thing arousing enthusiasm: modern furniture is a particular passion of Bill's.

2 (the Passion) the suffering and death of Jesus: meditations on the Passion of Christ. • a narrative of the Passion from any of the Gospels. • a musical setting of any of the narratives of the Passion: an aria from Bach's St. Matthew Passion.

ORIGIN Old English passion, from Latin passio(n-) (chiefly a term in Christian theology), from pati 'suffer'; subsequently reinforced by Old French.

New Oxford American Dictionary

3. passion - noun - as used about the Spirit World. – Humanella

• an intense desire or enthusiasm for something.

• a thing arousing enthusiasm.

New Oxford American Dictionary

Amorella: From now on, when we place new definitions for the Spirit World, we Bold them in this book. As the Reader observes, we are creating a Spirit World English Dictionary.

Richard: This is so awesome. I am super excited to be on this project. Bumdangers!

Amorella: Really, orndorff? Where did "bumdangers" come from?

Richard: I couldn't think of any expletive that would fit, so the word popped into my head. I am trying to understand what it means if it means anything – bum-dang-ers. I'll use it as my expletive from now on – being more polite yet laid back.

Was your question an order. Should I use "Yes, Ma'am"?

Amorella: What do you think, orndorff?

Richard: I feel better using: "Yes, Ma'am" when you give me an order-like statement.

Amorella: Follow what your heartansoulanmind is comfortable with. I'll politely correct you when you err.

Richard: Thank you, Amorella, that is an excellent response.

14 July 2023, Friday

Richard: I'm ready to begin Chapter Twenty-One. I am also tired, so I will wait until tomorrow.

Amorella: You are off the hook, orndorff, but don't become discouraged. You're not dead yet. Are you enjoying my wit?

Richard: That I am. You make me smile, Amorella; literally, you do. You are the Queen/King of Dark Humor. I'm going to bed early. I go pick up Carol from The Gables tomorrow, have lunch with Fritz, and head to Cathy and Tod's house for an afternoon conversation.

15 April 2023, Saturday

Amorella: As you awakened this morning, you had a flash thought from seemingly nowhere. A compromise on voice. Each chapter might be read by one of our two simulated AI voices that Richard and I chose as a compromise for the voice we would like to be associated with. Richard thought I ought to read the first chapter, and he the second, switching off every other chapter. I felt that if, in principle that each represents their own original sex, the Listener could choose which to read each chapter. The Listener may listen to Richard's simulated voice first and switch to every other chapter. For curiosity's sake, listen to each chapter twice, once with Richard, the Reader, and once with me, the Reader.

Richard: Or, the Listener may choose to listen to each voice however sheorhe chooses. Select your Reader with the Text-to-Speech voice the Listener feels is appropriate for each chapter, whichever voice fits the Listener. We respectfully accept you picking a voice or representative voices of those of your own ancestors to do our readings.

Amorella: We ask that you treat us politely and respectfully, as you would a good friend, because it is the words, the conversation between the more recently living and the long dead, that make this book worth its time and consideration in your life.

Amorella: You and Carol had a good time with Cathy, Tod, and your cousin Wendy, who stopped by for a visit. Unfortunately, you waited too long for ice cream, so you must make up for it on Saturday. Tod was in the living room, and Cathy and Carol

inspected Cathy's early bushes and flowers. Wendy arrived from across West Park Street. She is two years younger than Cathy.

While you were alone near the back door, she asked about Auntie Theo and Uncle Doc Haines. Wendy said she and Cathy went out to see Auntie, who lived up on East College at the time, and when they arrived, Auntie did not come to the door, but the vacuum sweeper was on while she slumped in a nearby chair. You did not know that she and Cathy were the first witnesses to Auntie Theo Haines' death.

Richard: I had never heard that family story before. I did not know Mom, Cathy, and Wendy discovered her from a front window because of the locked front door. Wendy had asked why Uncle Doc had the name because he was not a medical doctor. I told her that someone in the family told me he had been very good with various farm animals and their ailments. Cathy agreed with this assessment.

Younger neighbor farmers on Freeman Road and elsewhere asked about animal cures, and Doc Haines told them what worked without a charge. He was not formally certified, but he knew what he talked about regarding raising farm animals, dogs, and cats and caring for them. I understood that everyone liked and respected him for his caring personality and astute farming practices.

Amorella: You brought Auntie Theo and Uncle Doc up before, but your present story reminds me of those who were a vital part of their community but were not involved in politics or community leadership. People who were stable whether they had something that would put them in the local history books. Many old headstones and just plain stones that mark graves have under them; those bones were once filled with human dignity and worth, but who would have never thought of self-promotion because it was beneath their personal dignity.

Quiet, hardworking people on farms, in villages, in towns, and in cities everywhere. People have ancestors such as Auntie and Uncle Doc, unknowns to their families; however, they are always in the genes that carry on in the world. This fact is a reality, and nothing is remotely sentimental about their existence's personal practical, and spiritual memories.

Richard: That last sentence is a kicker, Amorella, and it brings a tear. The sentence balances the Romantic and Neo-classic literary thoughts of their day.

Amorella: Orndorff, ever the English major. You can't help yourself, old man. You are in the classroom either as a teacher or student and sometimes as the clean-up word custodian.

Richard: Sometimes, I need to catch your words, Amorella, but I love your quick wit. How this is, how this can be, that you, Amorella, exist as well as me.

Amorella: Two pods in a bean from where I have been.

Amorella: Before you stopped at Cathy and Tod's, you had lunch with Fritz; no fiasco at Bob Evans today. You two discussed local and national political issues, and you heard more about how the legal system works, about Fritz's brother Tim, and his

problems with falling, just as you do. Fritz got your note yesterday, and today, he wonders when you will finish this work, so he can read it as a whole work.

Richard: We two had laughs and smiles along lunch's way. I can't remember what they were about, and even if I could, they would mostly be inside jokes from knowing each other since the eighth grade. We have always gotten along. I don't remember us ever having an argument that was not resolvable in short order. Now that I think about it, I rarely argued with anyone. I'm talking a down-and-out shouting match, slamming doors, which Carol and I have had very few times in our marriage, but we have had them. I don't ever remember thinking about this before.

Maybe I have, if so, it is or was, written down at one time or another – and thrown away later also, as writing has been an anger management therapy for me . . . forever in my life. – I don't feel angry now, though. Isn't that odd? I am always angry about something, but I'm drawing a blank right now. Hopefully, that is a good thing.

Amorella: You are listening to Michael Silverman piano-playing "Walden Pond" as dusk floats up from the western horizon. The cats are asleep on separate chairs in the living room. A robin sits atop the pole holding about twenty-five percent of the seed.

Richard: There are more leaves out across all the old fence bushes. Spring is here. Leftover seed means the pre-momma birds are nesting and about to have babes. Well, that's an assumption.

Amorella: Do you have any other assumptions, orndorff?

Richard: I don't have any anger, and I don't have any other assumptions, Amorella. This is a relatively quiet evening in that sense. If you have anything, you want to discuss – have at it. I am open to almost anything.

Amorella: I'll take you at your word. Why discuss "almost anything;" I, the Amorella, am open to discussing anything.

Richard: I should have expected that question, but I didn't. You are right. For a split second, I hesitated before writing "almost." I don't know why I hesitated, but I did. If I thought of anything, my unconsciousness super-quickly avoided conscious detection. If my unconscious avoided the subject, there must have been a reason. Now, that is intriguing. Pause. Strangely, my intuition tells me that, in this case, my unconsciousness is not for my protection but for its own private reason.

Amorella: Orndorff, why would intuition do such a thing? Is it running a detective service of sorts?

Richard: You are projecting two independent personal characterizations onto my Unconsciousness and intuition when I assume the two are as a unit, so I am capitalizing the words. You have placed me into independent parts of consciousness for a few weeks.

All this leans toward the fact that my 'Self' is not into the 'Life of Self' on its own. Multiple personalities appear to be coming out of the woodwork. I should find this scary, but I don't. This question of me having multiple personalities is mildly interesting but without merit. I don't feel "scattered about."

You are putting a puzzle to me to solve when I don't even know what the image of the puzzle is, other than, perhaps, an overabundant Imagination (a third characterization) that would be more freaked out than tedious.

Amorella: For argument's sake, what you write above has a grain of truth. Then who is the 'you' in control of these bits and pieces – a more significant, independent part of the puzzle? This is not so. In fact, my spiritual intuition says it is a much smaller piece of mystery, hidden away, a part of yourself that you do not know exists. This mystery does, indeed, do most of the unconscious controlling you are referencing.

Richard: The first thing that comes to mind is someone like that little alien in my fiction. My mind always wants to withhold imagination from the escape-the-world table and substitute anything else for daydreaming my life away.

Amorella: Do you mean the Dreamland of the Australian Aboriginals rather than daydreaming?

Richard: I don't know. Here is what I found about *Dreamland* from Britannica dot com the Dreaming

Australian Aboriginal mythology

Written and fact-checked by the Editors of Encyclopaedia Britannica

"The Dreaming, also called dream-time or world dawn [in] Australian Aboriginal languages . . . a mythological period with a beginning but no foreseeable end, during which the natural environment was shaped and humanized by the actions of mythic beings. Many of these beings took the form of human beings or of animals ("totemic"); some changed their forms. They established the local social order and its "laws." Some, especially the great fertility mothers and male genitors, were responsible for creating human life—i.e., the first people.

Mythic beings of the Dreaming are eternal. Though in the myths, some were killed or disappeared beyond the boundaries of the people who sang about them, and others were metamorphosed as physiographic features (for example, a rocky outcrop or a waterhole) or manifested as or through ritual objects (see Tujunga), their essential quality remained undiminished. In Aboriginal belief, they are spiritually as alive today as ever. The places where the mythic beings performed some action or were "turned into" something else became sacred, and the ritual was focused around them.

Dreaming, as a coordinated system of belief and action, includes totemism. Together, they express a close relationship: man is regarded as part of nature, not fundamentally dissimilar to the mythic beings or animal species, all of which share a common life force. The totem serves as an agent, placing man within the Dreaming and providing him with an indestructible identity that continues uninterruptedly from the beginning of time to the present and into the future."

Selected from the Encyclopedia Britannica - britannica.com

Richard: What do I do with this material, Amorella?

Amorella: I will take from the above a few bits that relate to the way of the dead in this book. (You, Richard, are thinking ever critically, that this is an unlikely source.)

I, the Amorella, will make myself more straightforward after I do these cross-outs and major adjusting editing from above to directly below.

Amorella's editing from Britannica:

A. Dreaming is a coordinated system of belief and action.

B. The [soul] serves as an agent, placing people within the Dreaming and providing herorhim with an indestructible identity that continues uninterruptedly from the beginning of time to the present and into the future.

Amorella: The above words are allegorical in nature but give added character to what the soul is from the point of view of some of those heartsansoulsanminds physically dead. In this book, even the word 'heartansoulanmind' appears allegorical once one is physically dead. This promotes an understanding for the Living

to consider in their apprehensions and fears concerning physical death. This work is understanding and not knowledge-based. Take it or leave it.

Richard [surprised]: I agree with you, Amorella. This book promotes Understanding of what many believe about Heaven through their personal and community faith in G-D. This work is not set as an argument. *Something Is Eternal* is designated as an Understanding, a viewpoint. This book presents a more vital, modern human-oriented point of view of the Afterlife, which includes a coexisting human spirit, two Humanella in one, who once lived on Earth just as we Readers.

Amorella: This concludes the chapter.

OPEN

Chapter Twenty-one

17 April 2023, Monday

Amorella: When you awoke a little while ago, you thought of our conversation about the Aboriginals last night. The science fiction film about the translation of language popped into my mind as an analogy between octopus-type water creatures and human beings.

Richard: I need to remember the title. (It is remembered on the next page.)

Amorella: While searching for the film title, you came across "The Cambridge Declaration of Consciousness," which I would like you to include:

"The Cambridge Declaration of Consciousness"

"On 7 July 2012, a prominent international group of cognitive neuroscientists, neuropharmacologists, neurophysiologists, neuroanatomists, and computational neuroscientists gathered at The University of Cambridge to reassess the neurobiological substrates of conscious experience and related behaviors in human and non-human animals. . . ..

We declare the following: "The absence of a neocortex does not preclude an organism from experiencing affective states. Convergent evidence indicates that non-human animals have the neuroanatomical, neurochemical, and neurophysiological substrates of conscious states and the capacity to exhibit intentional behaviors. Consequently, the weight of evidence indicates that humans are not unique in possessing the neurological substrates that generate consciousness. Non-human animals, including all mammals and birds, and many other creatures, including octopuses, also possess these neurological substrates."

* The Cambridge Declaration on Consciousness was written by Philip Low and edited by Jaak Panksepp, Diana Reiss, David Edelman, Bruno Van Swinderen, Philip Low, and Christof Koch. The Declaration was publicly proclaimed in Cambridge, UK, on 7 July 2012, at the Francis Crick Memorial Conference on Consciousness in Human and non-Human Animals, at Churchill College, University of Cambridge, by Low, Edelman, and Koch. The Declaration was signed by the conference participants that evening, in the presence of Stephen Hawking, in the Balfour Room at the Hotel du Vin in Cambridge, UK. The signing ceremony was memorialized by CBS 60 Minutes."

Amorella: Reading your mind, I 'see' you would like there to be evidence that humans can go a step further, and you submit this book and all the notes from the 1980s plus, to show that it is possible to communicate with the spirit world rationally through a spirit such as myself.

Richard: Amorella, I would never share such an intimate conscious secret with anyone in a billion years. Why? It is self-serving. Yesterday, you stated,". . . those bones once filled with human dignity and worth, but who would have never thought of self-promotion, because it was beneath their personal dignity."

Amorella: This is why I brought it up; you, sometimes timid soul. It is self-serving this book, not yourself. Why? Because one part of you doesn't give a tinker's damn about the this book, one way or another. This is another piece of your "secret self" that allows this all to co-exist (consciously and unconsciously) in the first place.

Richard: I had not thought that. I should be angry with you, Amorella, but I find it strangely just like me to "not give a tinker's damn," which I, again, tip my beret in salute of the phrase to Clell Tuller Orndorff, my long-time grandfather.

Amorella: Look outside orndorff and see the new dawn. Every day begins with a new birth.

Richard: I still don't have the title of that octopus-oriented alien film, but enough for now. I need a break . . . *Arrival*, that's the title, distributed by Paramount Pictures.

Richard: This work or all my notes of a lifetime are not even circumstantial evidence of anything other than sometimes being earthbound and bored and having flights of imagination to go with it; that's the truth, Amorella.

Amorella: Reader: This is what I must put up with. Richard, sometimes, doesn't even give a tinker's damn about the sunrise. Wait until he doesn't see them anymore.

Richard: I am at Alum Creek Dam, looking north towards the pines. I just completed the last chapter (coming up next). This took me longer to go over than usual, but as always, it was something new that I never had in my life before, as far as I can recollect, consciously or unconsciously.

Amorella: You sound refreshed, old man. New concepts and ideas are challenging to take in sometimes. You couldn't imagine what the Aboriginal mythology could have anything to do with this work, even though you once (long ago and far away) discussed the Aboriginal myths in the public-school classroom in a class titled World Mythology as Literature.

Richard: I don't remember the exact title, but that was the intent. Literature. It was an elective, a quarter class for Juniors and Seniors at Indian Hill High School. It was more popular than I thought it would be. I don't know why. My lectures were somewhat dull, I suppose, but the students each gave presentations and facts about the myth of cultures from around the world. Students enjoyed the research and giving their presentations. Most everyone in the class was interested; no doubt because it was one of a series of department electives they could choose.

*Amorella: The cats have been fed. On the way home, you connected your heartansoulanmind to the old poetic device, personification. You think of your name as legal, which it is, but in the spirit world, one's chosen name after physical death becomes the human spirit's **poetic name**. Humanella mentioned some of this information in an earlier chapter.*

*The poetic name, may be why, after completing the task of moving through the phase I call **once-life**, the poetic name takes meaning on a short paragraph, which the living, if hearing one's chosen spirit world name, might sound like a minor poetic work, typically from a language's romantic or neoclassic period of literature. In other words, each human's name becomes a piece of spiritual poetry and it is their personal signature within the spirit world.*

If you add this personal signature as an allegorical statement, straight from one's heart of hearts, it rings good enough as a living human translation as well as new name among fellow human spirits.

There is no sound, no alphabet. It is an understanding as to who is who upon greeting. This concept, again, is allegorical in nature for the living. The words may gain acceptance as an understanding without nitpicking as to what is truth and what is not. Think of it as spiritual grammar sensing the logic, intellect, intensity and reasoned passion of the spirit next to you, and accept the fellow spirit with empathetic Understanding, if nothing else. Spirits rest but do not sleep, they contemplate and share themselves and their interests with other spirits as friends or acquaintances.

The Reverend Dr. Goss's contribution

Amorella: *First, I thank The Reverend Dr. John Douglas Goss for finding this material online and sharing. I am going to make use of it. Surprised, aren't you, orndorff?*

Richard: No, I am not, other than I can't believe Doug found this material; I didn't even know there was such a list. It is exciting reading and is undoubtedly a conversation starter, Amorella. Doug and I are on the same wavelength most of the time.

Amorella: I will react to each with a sentence. Remember, I am a spirit who once lived individually; my reaction will show this. Let's do them one at a time in order of presentation but without numbers attached. This selected work is from STARinsider.com.

*The title of the article's photographic display is **"30 theories about what happens when you die."** The editor's introduction to begin the piece is this:*

Note: I, the Amorella, alone, do the 'accepting' or 'not accepting commentary' in my addition to the article.

The Article from STARinsider.com
"30 theories about what happens when you die"

Introduction

For many people, the fear of death revolves around the fear of the unknown. What happens when we die? Do we go to heaven, get reincarnated into an animal, or re-programmed in the simulation? Narrowing down people's many theories about death, check out these philosophies about the afterlife!

The simulation theory: Does it ever feel like everything in life is programmed? What if death was? The simulation theory believes our lives are quantitative data in a higher being's video game.

Not accepted as written, Amorella

The Rastafarian theory Rastafarians believe that life is eternal. It is only those who shun righteousness that actually die. Because of this, funerals are not really celebrated in their culture.

Partial acceptance, Amorella

The never-ending life theory is definitely one of the most unique. This claims that when you die, you are immediately reborn into your life again without any memory of the life you had just led before.

Not accepted as written, Amorella

The cosmic theory claims that our consciousness belongs to the universe, not our individual bodies. Therefore, when you die, your consciousness returns to the cosmos.

Not accepted as written, Amorella

The Buddhist theory Buddhists believe in reincarnation after death. You can be reborn into different realms after death, whether a god, demi-god, human, animal, or ghost.

Not accepted as written, Amorella

The parallel universe theory The similar universe theory has been explained in countless sci-fi movies and comic books, but could it be real? This theory claims that when we die, we will be living in the same universe as we were before, just in a different portion of space and time.

Partially accepted as written, Amorella

The dream theory: What if it was all just a dream? The dream theory claims that when we die, we will just wake up from a very confusing, vivid, and long dream. Pinch yourself.

Not accepted as written, Amorella

The Aztec theory The ancient Aztec's view of the afterlife was separated into three paths: the sun, Mictlan, or Tlalocan. How you die determines your afterlife. Fallen soldiers and women who died giving birth became hummingbirds that followed the sun. People who died from a "less glorious" cause would go to Mictlan. And anyone who died by drowning went to Tlalocan.

Not accepted as written, Amorella

Plato's theory Plato believed that the physical world limited our knowledge and that when a person dies, they move on to a new, more fulfilling life. His theory was that death allows souls to find their actual existence.

Accepted as written, Amorella

The nothingness theory What if when we die, everything turns to pitch black, and you are gone forever? That is not exactly a comforting thought.

Not accepted as written, Amorella

The Mormon theory The Church of Latter-Day Saints believes that excellent and righteous Mormons become gods when they die. Alternatively, non-believers are condemned to the afterlife.

Not accepted as written, Amorella

The Egyptian pharaoh theory Egyptian pharaohs believed that death was impermanent. For this reason, mummification was essential to preserve the body for its second life.

Not accepted as written, Amorella

The uncertain theory All we know about death is what happens to the physical body. The uncertain theory addresses this cold reality while leaving the rest up for debate.

Debatable as written, Amorella

The paranormal theory This theory is usually the backbone of most horror films. Those who believe in the paranormal claim that our souls remain among the living on Earth after death. It is also often felt that communication with these souls is possible through various mediums.

Rarely accepted as written, Amorella

The Hindu theory of Hinduism also holds the belief in reincarnation. A person's status or form in the next life.

Rarely accepted as written, Amorella

The egocentric theory: Do you think you are the center of the universe? If so, the egocentric view of death may be just for you! This theory claims that the universe starts with your birth and ends with your death.

Not accepted as written, Amorella

The 'Stranger Things theory If you have seen the hit Netflix series Stranger Things' then you know what Upside Down is.

The show claims an alternate dimension to our universe that a person can become trapped in, being neither alive nor dead.

Not accepted as written, Amorella

The frozen head theory Some people believe that by freezing themselves after death, they will be preserved for the future. They may still be alive, just very, very cold.

Not accepted as written, Amorella

The solipsism theory: Does anything outside of your mind really exist? The solipsism theory is valid in both life and death. The only thing we can definitively say is real is what an individual sees and experiences. So, when the individual dies, everything else does as well.

Not accepted as written, Amorella

The excretion theory claims that the universe is a giant brain in the human body, and individuals are merely cells. Therefore, when a cell dies in the human body, it gets excreted, which is what happens to people.

Not accepted as written, Amorella

The Christian theory Christians believe in both Heaven and Hell. If a person is good and righteous, they will enter the utopia that is Heaven. However, they will end up in Hell if they lead a life of sin and wrongdoings.

Not accepted as written, Amorella

The nihilist theory Nihilism deems that all values are meaningless and baseless. An authentic nihilist way of approaching death and the afterlife is that there is nothing afterward because even life has nothing.

Not accepted as written, Amorella

The 'Beetlejuice' theory The hit Tim Burton film 'Beetlejuice' revolves around a recently deceased couple haunting their old home and its new owners. The only way to be freed from this middle dimension is if an iconoclast exorcist frees you. Would you like the afterlife to be like this 1988 comedy?

Partially, and rarely accepted as written, Amorella

The pessimist theory Perhaps this conversation is moot because we are already dead? That's what the pessimist theory believes, anyway.

Not accepted as written, Amorella

The many worlds theory claims that when we die, we only die in this one current universe. There are other universes out there for us to move on to.

Rarely accepted as written. Amorella

The illusion theory claims that the world is created more in our minds than in a literal sense, meaning it is all an illusion. Following this understanding, death is a human-constructed concept, and when we die, we still remain.

Not acceptable as written, Amorella

'The Good Place' theory is Another viral TV idea of the afterlife. The hit series 'The Good Place' follows the main characters accidentally let into Heaven, also known as "The Good Place."

Full of frozen yogurt, custom houses, and your true soulmate, many viewers hope this fictional philosophy is true.

Not accepted as written, Amorella

The levels theory What if being a human being was just the first level of existence? The levels theory claims that we move on from our initial form when we die.

Partially accepted as written, Amorella

The Tree Theory Have you ever heard of the Tree of Life? Some people take that literally by having their remains buried in a tree pod. This way, your body is returned to the Earth, and you may become a proud tree in your next existence.

Not accepted as written, Amorella   **[End of Article]**

Richard: I am surprised that Plato's concept is only one acceptable. Why?

Amorella: Plato's concept fits a reasonable structure of thought throughout. Therefore, it is acceptable.

18 April 2023, Monday

Richard: I have a question for **Humanella.** . When you were a single once-human spirit was your soul an original?

Humanella: What a curious question.

Richard: I didn't think through the question. Sorry.

Humanella: *Are you asking if my soul has always been my soul?*

Richard: Yes, when your soul took in your male friend.

Humanella: *Both souls attach, in a figurative sense – think magnets.*

Richard: I thought you would say attached, like a hug.

Humanella: *Think about it, orndorff.*

Richard: I need clarification, please. Is each spirit just the head and face?

Humanella: *Each is as a face, like my other half. A true-looking ghost would be like herorhis face in life – at whatever age you wanted the face to be. I figuratively dressed up for the occasion.*

Richard: You have your humanity.

Amorella: *What good would I be without, Sir Richard.*

Richard: That last comment, Sir Richard, reminds me of my old friend and colleague at Mason City Schools, Laney Bender Slack; she sometimes called me 'Sir Richard.' We were close friends for twenty-five years of our lives. I called her 'm'Lady.' People move on in their lives. We did.

Humanella: *Like you and your old college friend, Bert Fields.*

Richard: Friends, yes. Otherwise, no. my relationships with Bert and Laney are both unique, just like will all other friends. A one-on-one friendship is always unique.

Humanella: *Of course. All personal friendships are unique, even in the Spirit World.*

Richard: Laney is a professor at the Catholic university in Cincinnati, Xavier. Dr. Laney Bender Slack teaches education classes and some university extensions in Peru. She and her husband, Jay, also has his doctorate in another field, both are professionals. They have two grown children. I am trying to remember their names presently. Laney always helped me out when I couldn't remember colleagues' names. Laney was kind enough to buy me a book for Christmas when we first worked together. I am trying to remember if I got her anything. I mean, we were friends already. She didn't have any children yet. We worked together in the Department of English at Mason High School.

Laney went to Bowling Green State University as an undergraduate, and I decided to go to BGSU for my Master's in Education so we had that in common. We quickly became friends as well as colleagues. As an undergraduate, she student-taught at the American school in Rio de Janeiro.

I taught at Escola Graduada in Sao Paulo, so we had that connection too. Those, easily shared memories brought us closer together. Laney also taught our daughter, Kim, seventh-grade English when at Mason. I met Laney earlier when Kim was in her class, Kim was our first personal connection.

When Kim had Laney for class, I immediately took a liking to Laney because she was young, bright, cheerful, and enthusiastic about teaching. Laney made me feel good about the future of teacher education. The book she gave me for Christmas was *The Complete Works of William Shakespeare.* I have the text stored at Kim's house now. Owen or Brennan might come to use it.

Laney and I didn't always agree on how to teach our classes, but we were tolerant of one another. One of the differences was that I enjoyed lecturing and having students take notes. She worked with her students in small groups and had great discussions. She was one of the best things to happen to me while teaching at Mason, especially when she moved to the high school to teach English.

I had male friends like Gary Poppelwell, another best friend, but very few female friends that I consciously and unconsciously found myself attached to outside of fellow English teacher, Angie Edmonds. Laney and I still converse now and then. She is a busy woman. Laney is a kind and caring person in and out of the classroom.

Humanella: *You had a lot to say, orndorff. I am not surprised, though. Laney is a deeper friend in your heart.*

Richard: That is very kind of you, Humanella. . I am surprised sometimes.

Humanella: *Are you surprised I can be kind and caring also?*

Richard: This suddenly feels very awkward. I need a break.

Humanella: *Go to it, old man orndorff.*

Richard: You are sounding a lot like Amorella with your commentary.

Humanella: *To keep the record straight, Laney inspired Friendly's character in your published trilogy. Is that correct?*

Richard: Yes, she did, but other colleagues from different schools also inspired characters. Mainly through their faces and personalities, the characters are composites of many people I have known. Angie Edmonds, re-composed became a model for Hartolite, sometimes called Hart, also a Marsupial character. The two appear in dialogues in the story just as you and I do, Amorella. This is too much of a coincidence.

Humanella: *Yes, it is. You are creating this dialogue through the flow of different areas of your heartansoulanmind. You are, in a sense, your own coincidence, orndorff. This is funny.*

Richard: This 'coincidence' is either idiosyncratic, eccentric, or neither; I don't know which.

Humanella: *Take your pick.*

Richard: I'll stick with my first choice, idiosyncratic. I selected and edited the definition below from Wikipedia because the intention is broader than usual dictionaries.

Idiosyncrasy

An idiosyncrasy is an unusual feature of a person (though there are also other uses; see below). It can also mean an odd habit. The term is often used to express eccentricity or peculiarity. A synonym may be "quirk."

Etymology

Idiosyncrasy, "a peculiar temperament, habit of the body" (from . . . "blend of the four humors" (temperament)) or literally "particular mingling."

New Oxford American Dictionary

Richard: My intuition tells me "particular mingling" fits more concisely than coincidence. I have never seen this combination of two words before. The word has not, either. Grammarly says the sentences are not long enough to create a score but shows nothing wrong with the word choice in a sentence. As such, I feel "coincidence" should be replaced with "particular mingling."

Amorella suddenly returns: *I disagree; however, you have your rebuttal. Let's drop this into the chapter.*

Richard: Fine with me, Amorella. This chapter appears somewhat long with more than three thousand words.

Amorella: I am not bound by numbers, orndorff.

Richard: I understand, Ma'am. Thank you. [Relief. I am not bound by numbers either.]

OPEN

Chapter Twenty-two

20 April 2023, Tuesday

Richard: Amorella sent this as a Note to my iPhone last night:

Amorella: Richard, you are an innocent man. How can that be? Because everyone has some innocence in them. I understand this. Otherwise, why are people forgiven? I, the Amorella, call a spade a spade.

It is a built-in innocence a person has. Unconscious innocence, if you will. This is only when sheorhe understands why sheorhe is forgiven. This is why the recent dead think things out – who they were in life and are as a human spirit. No living human is entirely innocent of anything. We are talking spiritual levels here because, Richard, you are hypothetically dead.

The more honest the living person is, sheorhe can better witness dishonesty in others. If the person who is recently dead is dishonest, sheorhe is in for a hell of a road trip through a spiritual fantasy land.

I see you from the inside first, orndorff, then outside – that's how it is. You have the honesty to know who you are while living. That's the reason you are chosen for this work. You are an example of honesty, nothing more, nothing less. Capiche?

Richard: I feel I understand, but then I don't, because I don't know what honesty is; that is, to define honesty to my satisfaction. Thank you, Amorella.

267

[I like that Amorella puts everything in a straight-lines for me. I appreciate it, and I understand it. But, more importantly, I wholeheartedly accept my honesty without fully understanding what honesty is when I am being honest. Now, I just need to shut up and get some sleep. Thank you, Amorella.]

Amorella: I'm glad you clarified that last paragraph, orndorff. You are not a joke, old man.

Richard: Thank you, again, Amorella. Sometimes I don't know what a joke is. Some jokes can be more fun, some, not. This is one of the many reasons I could have never been a scholar. I was not scholarly material I understood this in junior high and high school.

Richard: Some people cannot help the classification other people put them in. I understand this fully well. People accept what other people tell them mostly without question. I like to question almost everything, privately, of course. Adults tell kids things that stick with the children their entire lives, and they never learn, wish, or care to question their parents or anyone else; or some go the other way and, almost with a boast, question everything anyone says. One doesn't have to think to question people or situations, that's my point. - rho

I *do* question myself sometimes. It is human. I wonder why we do things every day without a thought. Why? Because thinking. and not always thinking critically, is something we don't have time to do because, I feel we are conditioned to be busy little beavers. Sometimes busyness should be declared a sin, the opposite of sloth, it is as a sin to me. This world is full of busyness that is brought on, and that is not necessary to have a full life. That's my opinion.

Meanings take on a person's character. Not all meanings are real. This means some of a person's character (their reality themselves) is not truthful either. Some people are afraid to think like I am here. I don't know what people are afraid of. I've survived my whole life thinking the way I do. I am comfortable with it. However, this means I am also only *sometimes* comfortable with other people and their outward behaviors. I accept this. No argument from me. Why? This is part of who I am.

Amorella: Orndorff, you show an example of what the dead know to be true in their present condition – living consciously with only a sense of self and consciousness. This is a very good reason why honesty is essential. You don't need to think about it because scrutinizing is an example of what you are.

Richard: I need to take on faith that you are correct. As such, I am curious to know whether you are right in your assumption about what we discussed that I have forgotten.

Amorella: This is what I am talking about, orndorff.

Richard: I am not writing what I want to write about; I am writing what you want to write about. Please recognize these are my honest thoughts. I would not be so impolite in real life, but I am supposed to be dead, so all I have are my thoughts.

Amorella: What do you want to write about?

Richard: I want answers before I know how to word the questions.

Amorella: Isn't that a rather self-centered and selfish attitude?

Richard: I am the center of myself – what do you expect me to be? I don't think this is selfish. It is efficient. I wouldn't impose on you, on your time or timelessness for something frivolous, and I would not expect you to impose the frivolousness on me.

Amorella: This still sounds self-centered to me.

Richard: Fuck you, Amorella. I don't give a shit what it sounds like to you. So – there. Are you satisfied?

Amorella: Yes, I am. This is an example of honesty in action. This is orndorff to the core. – 'fuck you, Amorella.' Honesty is what it is; and most of the time, it is not polite. In this situation, Richard doesn't 'give a shit' about being polite. He is angry and pissed off because I can provoke it. This is the real orndorff.

Richard does care. These pages show he cares very much about the world and its people. He cares about the spiritual world and wants to be on top of it when the time comes. He doesn't want to waste time on 'tra-lee-laa shit.' What does he want?

He wants the world to be a better place to raise children, and he wants everyone to be healthy to work they like to do like he did. He wants everyone to respect one another and be polite and honest with everyone whenever possible, which in this world, it is not.

He hates the world for what it is in that sense, and his only solution is for everyone to do something about it without destroying everything good and humane. It is easier to say, "fuck it, Amorella." He's an efficient ass, so that's why he says it. That's my tra-lee-laa shit, not his. Let's end the chapter.

Richard: Yes, Ma'am. Thank you, Amorella. Your talk has been reasonable. I'm satisfied, but a little displeased with myself. Angry issues. I'm not going to apologize. Amorella, you much more intelligent than me, and I respect you. I appreciate intelligence, wisdom, and patience from anyone.

I'm not the smartest kid on the block. I get confused when people don't speak clearly and distinctly, and I don't like it when I don't speak or write clearly also. I'm stubborn with a chip on my shoulder. No excuses. That's who I am. Take it or leave it. I'm not going to change for you, Amorella, or anyone else. I'm an old man who has been using old man ways for a lifetime. You already said it was the 'end of the chapter.' I desired to be polite and respectful, but I had something else to say.

Amorella: Being stubborn is like running through a briar patch naked. No good comes from it, and not much blood is let, but the scars can itch terribly while healing. So, keep that in mind when you're stubborn.

Richard: A lot of old people would like to be beneficial to society. I've been a lucky man, and I have had a good life, a good partner/wife, good friends and family who I love. I loved life, my better experiences, and a lot of the people. I have known some very kind souls in life. What's better than knowing some kind souls wherever you are?

Amorella: What's that all about?

Richard: Well, I'm supposed to be dead so I thought I would say something appropriate to the Living. Being a teacher, I seemed nearly always talking. It was not the best classroom habit. I am quieter now. Writing is easier than speaking, because I have time to think and compose first.

20 April 2023, Thursday

Richard: I am respective of Angels if they exist, and I am respectful the Spirit of G-D. I am humbled before either. I am an old man afraid of nothing spiritual, but if demons exist as they did biblically, I want nothing to do with them. Thank you very much.

Amorella: I have an enlightened heartansoulanmind in hand. A torch like on the Statue of Liberty. I appreciate the honesty and foresightfulness, orndorff.

Richard: I need to find out whether you are Amorella or Humanella. Please let me be communicating with the Amorella I have known for forty years.

Amorella: You are arrogant, orndorff. Would you rather be communicating with the Spirit of G-D?

Richard: I am not always arrogant. I am human, and I don't know who else to reason with within this spiritual circumstance. I am respectful, and I expect respect for my heartansoulanmind in return. Pause. – Humbly, as a heartansoulanmind, I will talk with whoever will listen. I am at ease. My anger subsided. I wish to be wise. I am a human being with a heartansoulanmind, just like most every other. I am nothing else in the universe and Beyond, but I am not afraid of Being, either alive or physically dead.

Amorella: Good. You are not afraid. Above all, you are honest to the depths. If someone else spiritually minded has read this book, and wants to converse with you politely and reasonably, would you allow this?

Richard: Your words show you are Amorella. Rarely, if ever. I am old. I am not so patient and polite as I once was.

Amorella: You are a decent though very private man. You chose to publish with iUniverse, because you have successfully worked with them before. I am not done with you, orndorff. We have another book to complete, and another after that if you live long enough.

Richard: Thank you, Amorella-of-the-Forty-Years. I don't want you to leave me. You give me the courage to speak my heartansoulanmind. For this, I am forever grateful.

Amorella: On this rainy day, you are down at the park facing the Alum Creek dam. Carol and you had a Graeter's after picking her up, then you went home, snuggled for a half hour, climbed out of bed, and watched the birds from the Lanai. You had her back to The Gables by three-fifteen. Stopped, bought a McD's Diet Coke, and drank from it after finishing two cookies Carol forgot to take

in with her. You will park east a couple of spots and face the pines. Ready to continue writing?

Richard: You would think I would have some questions after this late morning's writing, but I don't, not presently, anyway. I am pleased. I have decided not to have anything to do with initiating anything. – Right now, this whole thing about speaking to readers is beginning to embarrass me very much. I responded. Rarely.

Amorella: I wondered how you would tackle the whole problem. I know it took a lot of faith to send that material to Hebrew Union back in the day. Your job and your reputation were on the line when you were young enough that it could have ended your career. You were not even an active church member anywhere, let alone Jewish even in discovered genetic background. Nevertheless, I sent you to Hebrew Union, and you followed through.

This book is not solicitation material. The world is full of solicitation to or for one thing or another. Like it or not, plenty of people of different faiths would shun the very idea of this piece of work. Leave this to the church or synagogue or temple or mosque, and what does the church or synagogue or temple or mosque have to lose and gain?

Humanella: I need to say: "Damn to anyone who solicits this material in a non-sacred manner." That sounds like the old days, doesn't it? In this book, no one damns anyone for anything without damning themselves first. This is not polite, but I still have the decency to be human in principle alone.

Richard: That woke me up. I see why there are two 'ellas', Amorella and Humanella

Amorella: Take a break, Richard. We can write later, or tomorrow.

Richard: Publishing one's heartansoulanmind is frightfully difficult, particularly for my being a deeply private man. (Pause) Being old makes it easier.

Amorella: It suddenly dawns on Richard that, <u>Something Is Eternal</u>, is much like a personal Declaration of Independence.

Richard: Yes, you worded it better than I.

Amorella: Readers, thank you for your time and patience. The Epilogue is next.

Epilogue

Amorella: *Richard is sitting in the car with his and Carol's gravestone about fifteen feet to the north while he is facing west. Richard pulls over enough that a vehicle can pass without an interruption. An unconscious notion suggests Richard back out of the spot and drive elsewhere. Another even earlier notion sent him here in the first place. Richard has many lifetime memories of this cemetery. Some memories were sad but not for a lifetime. When he was young this cemetery was Orndorff's playground; and even after he understood the 'meaning and the presence' of the dead. No one is rising, Orndorff, nor are you about to crumble over dead. Such an imagination Richard has.*

For orndorff, even without a capital, this personally space is hallowed ground, a natural place for his ashes one day. With that said, I, the Amorella, give this invocation: "Blessed may this world be for as long as humanity exists."

*Orndorff openly and quietly weeps for reasons he does not fully understand. This blessing is for everyone, for everyone's unselfish human kindness I find scattered about on this planet; nothing more, nothing less. Readers, enjoy life, keep it sacred, for personal consciousness is sacred whether it is recognized as such or not, at least in this book. – **The Amorella of the Forty Years***

Afterword

Amorella: I, Amorella, like Craig Brelsford's choice of words describing me as "simulated character dialogue" in the Foreword because it is an accurate description of myself. I am an invented color. It is a necessary choice. However, the words of The Amorella are as honest as Richard is within this book.

To our Readers

Individual human beings are contingent beings; they can their bodies, brains, personalities, and their heartsansoulsanminds, to different behaviors than they are because people have the free will to change their behaviors to be someone other than who they are in their present selves; someone less selfish, someone less angry, to be someone kinder and more helpful for the benefit of children and humankind.

As a spirit of many, The Amorella exist through spiritual necessity. We do not have the free will to change. The Amorella are perceptive and have the emotional intellect to respond and react to other spirits in other situations. My environmental position within Richard is normalized because I am always in touch with The Group, and they are always in touch with me.

It is interesting to be within a human heartansoulanmind, because I am generally created for witnessing and guiding those recently physically dead. I am placed within their heartsansoulsanminds to assist in the recent spiritual loss of the physical body. From my standpoint, this inclusive environment is within my range, except that Richard still has his physical self as I write from heartansoulanmind through his fingertips. His physical body is sensed but not observable to me. I 'read and write' from within Richard's humanity, his heartansoulanmind.

Readers, we thank you. - ***The Amorella***

OPEN

Printed in the United States
by Baker & Taylor Publisher Services